Crawford County Library District
Bourbon • Cuba • Steelville

2,000 MILES TO OREGON

AMERICA'S WESTWARD JOURNEY

JAMES J. FISHER • DON IPOCK

MONROE DODD

Kansas City Star Books

Based on a series of articles in *The Kansas City Star*
entitled "Tracing the Trail,"
written by James J. Fisher, illustrated by Don Ipock
and edited by Darryl W. Levings.

Editor, *2000 Miles to Oregon*: Monroe Dodd
Design: Jean Donaldson Dodd

Published by Kansas City Star Books
1729 Grand Boulevard, Kansas City, Missouri 64108

All rights reserved
Copyright © 2002 Kansas City Star Books

No part of this book may be reproduced, stored in a retrieval system, or transmitted in any form or by any means, electronic, mechanical, photocopying, recording or otherwise, without the prior consent of the publisher.

First Edition
Library of Congress Control Number: 2002106371

ISBN 0-9717080-7-X

Printed in the United States of America
by Walsworth Publishing Co., Inc.
Marceline, Missouri

Cover: Ruts on the Barlow Road, a portion of the Oregon Trail in Oregon.

Introduction photos
i: Depression left by overland trail caravans in a field, Pottawatomie County, Kan.
ii-iii: Tracks along the Sublette Cutoff, southwest Wyoming.
v: Near the trail's crossing of Rock Creek in southeast Nebraska.
viii: Reconstructed wagon, Rock Creek Station State Historical Park, Jefferson County, Neb.

CONTENTS

Introduction vii

About This Book ix

Setting Out 1

Prairie 10

High Plains 28

Plodding Along 34

Fort Laramie 45

Independence Rock 50

Toward the Divide 56

South Pass 60

Cutoff — or Not? 66

Bear River Valley 72

Indians 76

Snake River 79

Blue Mountains 87

The Whitmans 91

Columbia River 96

Barlow Road 103

Trail's End 108

Afterword 115

The West as it was known in 1846. This map, published in Philadelphia, showed the "Emigrant Route from Missouri to Oregon," and displayed a table of mileages to various points along it.

INTRODUCTION

Americans' dreams about the Pacific Northwest were first stirred more than two centuries ago, in 1792, when the Boston-based *Columbia* sailed into the river that became its namesake.

More than a decade later President Thomas Jefferson commissioned an expedition to reach this new country. Meriwether Lewis and William Clark were to cross the territory purchased in 1803 from France — the Louisiana Purchase, a vast empire of land stretching from the Mississippi River to the Rocky Mountains — and continue beyond it to the Columbia River and the Pacific. They made it across the continent and back, and their achievement burnished the popular image of the western country. It suggested that American civilization could cross the continent, too.

Through the first three decades of the 19th century the United States gradually spread west, from the Atlantic Coast, across the Appalachian Mountains, down the Ohio River, up the Mississippi River and across it. Then in the 1840s events combined to force some Americans to try to make real the dreams of the Pacific Northwest, and to do it immediately. Hard times, the prospect of free land, ambition and restlessness spurred Americans to make the leap beyond U.S. territory, beyond the formidable mountain ranges and all the way to the Pacific Coast. Their goal was the Columbia River region — Oregon country, a vaguely defined, faraway land claimed by the United States and Great Britain both.

These American emigrants first made their way to the farthest outpost in "The States." In the early 1840s that was Missouri. At the state's western edge, the Missouri River bent north, and westward trails began from Independence and Westport. From there the path to the Northwest crossed streams and prairie and plain, ascended mountain ranges and descended rivers. Jefferson hoped that Lewis and Clark would find a trade route to the Pacific, yet the place where they crossed the Continental Divide, in the Bitterroot Mountains of the Rockies, was too difficult for caravans. Many of the new emigrants were moving as families, carrying all their possessions, so they took an easier path through the mountains at a place called South Pass, named to distinguish it from Lewis and Clark's more northerly cut. The route traveled by these families became known as the Road to Oregon — the Oregon Trail — and the migration through the decade of the '40s signaled the start of an American epic.

In 1848, gold was discovered in California and the equation changed. Beginning in 1849, travelers along the trail numbered not in the thousands but in the tens of thousands. Most of these new emigrants were individuals, most of them motivated not by the chance to work and build a new life, but to get rich instantly. The jumping-off point moved north, up the Missouri River, so eager travelers could trim miles off their overland trek. After 1849, the vast majority of travelers along the trail broke off after crossing the Rockies and headed south to California.

These pages concentrate on the first decade of the migration, the 1840s, when more than 11,000 dreamers are estimated to have made the arduous trip from western Missouri across a broad district called Indian Territory to Oregon country for the purpose of starting over and the hope of a better life.

The dream lives on. Today, more than a century and a half later, the Pacific Northwest still holds a special place in the American culture and the American imagination. This is how that dream was first fulfilled.

About This Book

2,000 Miles to Oregon is based on a series of articles written by James J. Fisher, illustrated with photographs by Don Ipock and published in *The Kansas City Star*. The series, which marked the 150th anniversary of the first large body of emigrants to make the journey, was entitled "Tracing the Trail: Independence to Oregon." For this book those articles have been edited, supplemented and updated, and new photographs have been added. Also added have been details from two maps of the era. One is a map of the western part of North America printed in Philadelphia in 1846. The other, issued the same year, is a seven-map set based on expeditions by John Charles Fremont in 1842 and 1843 and printed at the behest of Congress. It was much used by emigrants.

To capture the immensity of the trek, this book shows the number of miles traveled by the caravans at various points in their journey. These are approximations of mileages determined by Aubrey L. Haines, who was commissioned by the National Park Service in 1972 to make its initial Oregon Trail Survey. In the 1980s part of Haines' report was reprinted in book form by the Patrice Press in *Historic Sites Along The Oregon Trail*. Distances are from Independence and Westport, and are based on the most frequently used route of the 1840s. That route began by following the paths worn by Santa Fe traders headed southwest. Near present-day Gardner in Johnson County, Kan., the Oregon travelers turned north, proceeding northwest along the valleys of the Kansas and Blue rivers and joining the Platte River. The valley of the Platte and its tributary, the Sweetwater, took them to the Continental Divide. After passing a few smaller rivers, the caravans met the Snake River. The Oregon Trail followed it and the Columbia River to the Willamette Valley.

To reflect the humanity of the emigrants, this book contains quotations from the contemporary diaries and later reminiscences of people who traveled the trail. They used far different conveyances and crude technology — and they wore clothing different from ours — but they experienced the same range of emotions and aspirations as we do today.

To capture what emigrants saw on their journeys, the new photographs show sites documented to have been on the Oregon Trail. They avoid modern intrusions as much as possible. Nevertheless fence posts, crops, trees and roads sometimes interject themselves in these images. Particularly on its eastern and western ends, the Oregon Trail has been much changed by human beings and their machines in the last century and a half.

Setting Out

> "ALL AGES AND SECTS ARE FOUND TO UNDERTAKE THIS LONG, TEDIOUS AND EVEN DANGEROUS JOURNEY…AND WHY? BECAUSE THE HUMAN MIND CAN NEVER BE SATISFIED, NEVER AT REST, ALWAYS ON THE STRETCH FOR SOMETHING NEW, SOME STRANGE NOVELTY."
>
> – James Clyman, 1846

The earliest emigrants gathered in western Missouri — men, women and children camped out in springtime beginning in the early 1840s.

They had this in common: They had caught the fever. They were going to the Pacific Northwest, a vast and ill-defined land called Oregon, a land of milk and honey.

What lay ahead of them was only vaguely discerned — more than 2,000 miles of dust and backbreaking work, endless horizons, disease and the consignment of loved ones to shallow graves, and panoramas most could not have imagined.

For more than two decades, tens of thousands of souls left outfitting and jumping-off places named Independence, Westport, St. Joseph, Fort Leavenworth, Nebraska City and Council Bluffs. They headed west, in the 1840s for Oregon and later to Utah and California, in wagons, on horses, but mostly on foot. It was a seminal event in the American experience.

Before the 19th century ended, those waves of emigrants would fill in the blank spaces on the maps of one quarter of the country, sweep aside the aboriginal Indians, see the land crisscrossed with rails and telegraph wires, and establish the political divisions and place names that exist to this day.

The pioneers who headed for the Oregon

Facing page: More than a century and a half ago a row of humble buildings stood at the base of this bluff beside the Missouri River, greeting would-be emigrants to Oregon as they disembarked from river steamers to begin their overland journey. From this place, Wayne City landing, the travelers ascended the bluff and made their way more than three miles to Independence. Many other emigrants in the early years of the Oregon Trail landed 10 miles upstream at the Kansas or Westport landing, not far from the mouth of the Kansas River, and headed four miles south to the town of Westport.

Setting Out

country in the 1840s peacefully pushed back Great Britain's claim to the Northwest. No other conquest of so much space has ever been accomplished with so little military force, political leadership or organized direction.

Although the heyday of the overland migration lasted only from 1840 to the mid-1860s, the migration over them set in motion events that transformed a weak nation into a power with a perceived destiny. Freedom became a commonplace of everyday life instead of a debated abstraction.

The road to Oregon was first traveled by white men in 1812, then forgotten, then rediscovered in 1824. Trappers and explorers and even a handful of early emigrants knew that it went west from Missouri to the Blue River Valley in Indian Territory, then to the Platte River. And the Platte watershed went to South Pass, the break through the Rocky Mountains. And onward many more miles to the Pacific.

A score of emigrants left Missouri in 1841. More than a hundred departed in 1842. By 1843

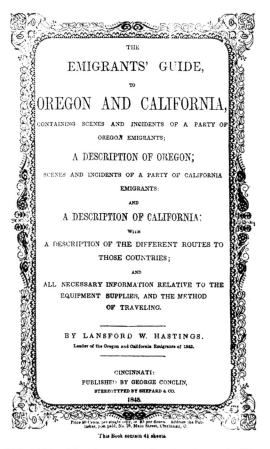

This 1845 publication promoted emigration to the West.

more than 800 were on the move. They would transform the road to Oregon into a highway.

More than anything physical, however, the words "Oregon Trail" conjured up an idea. Those words spawned wildly enthusiastic emigration societies all over and brought people boiling into the Missouri River towns.

"An April restlessness, a stirring of the blood, a wind from beyond the oaks' openings, spoke of the prairies, the great desert, and the Western Sea," wrote Bernard DeVoto. "The common man fled westward. A thirsty land swallowed him insatiably. There is no comprehending the frenzy of American folk migration. God's gadfly had stung us mad."

Through April and into May in those early years the groups straggled into Independence, or to the river landing upstream that led to Westport. Those Jackson County outfitting towns buzzed with sound and sights. This description of Independence in the 1840s was written by William G. Johnston:

"Noise and confusion reigned supreme. Traders, trappers and emigrants filled the streets and stores. All were in a hurry, jostling one another .... Mules and oxen strove for the right of way … while the loud cracking of ox goads,

Setting Out

squeaking of wheels and rattling of chains, mingled with the oaths of teamsters, produced a din indescribable."

The reign of Independence and Westport as starting points declined in the 1850s. Then emigrants began to realize that as much as 200 miles — that is, up to 18 days' travel and several ugly river crossings — could be cut off the trek by sticking longer with the northwest-bound Missouri River steamboats. The traffic began shifting upriver to Weston and Fort Leavenworth, to St. Joseph, to Nebraska City and Council Bluffs.

From all those places' dusty streets, people set out, some filled with a spirit of adventure, others with almost quaking fear.

And the question remains: Why did they go?

Why would whole families dare what some then called "palpable homicide" by setting out on a 2,000-mile journey into a wild and desolate land?

Some wanted to rid themselves of debt, and others wanted lush pastures. Others admitted they had been hooked by the propagandists

Trail commerce helped the landing for Westport grow in the 1850s, when it incorporated as the Town of Kansas.

Men and Women

In the 1840s, when social roles were more rigid than today, men inevitably made the decision about moving west. Single men were free to go as they wished; men with families could take their wife and children along or leave them at home. By the norms of the day, women had to accede, and so when they traveled they nearly always went as part of a family. Scholar Lillian Schlissel studied the diaries and reminiscences of 103 women who made the overland journey for her book, *Women's Diaries of the Westward Journey*. Comparing them with the accounts of men, she discovered clear differences in outlook between the sexes. Men, for one, expressed more optimism about the outcome of the journey; women directly or indirectly exhibited reservations about the possibility of success. Women were more charitable in their description of the Indians they came upon. Indeed, Schlissel found, women saw more clearly than men that the biggest dangers to travelers were disease and accidents.

A journey this difficult was for the young. Most emigrants were 16 to 30 years old and the vast majority were under 50.

Setting Out

who portrayed Oregon as a nirvana. Others, their diaries show, sought better health, or patriotic or political consideration. Still others showed a desire to get away from the sticky question of slavery, or a weariness of society's artificialities, or, in some cases, a wish to elude pursuing lawmen.

Some itched from the bite of "God's gadfly," citing boredom and a desire to do something more than walk behind a mule. Probably the most honest admitted that they wanted to "better" their lot, an ambition that Americans still hold dear.

"The people of this brief golden age were gross materialists and lofty idealists at the same time," wrote historian Bruce Catton. "They never imagined there might be a difference between economic freedom and political freedom. All that mattered was a fair

Not far from Independence, Archibald Rice built this house on his farm in 1844. It became a campsite for trail travelers bound for Oregon, California or Santa Fe. The home stands today at 66th Street and Blue Ridge Boulevard in Raytown, Mo.

chance to get them.

"Today was better than yesterday and tomorrow would be better than today. All horizons were open.... "

15 MILES

The first major stream crossing for travelers leaving Independence was the Blue River. After clambering up the stream's western bank, the caravans faced this rise. The depression in the ground, called a swale, was created over the years by wagon wheels, human feet and animal hooves struggling uphill. This and other swales are still visible in Minor Park, south and east of Red Bridge and Holmes roads in southern Kansas City, Mo.

Setting Out

Once the grass was up, providing food for animals, the wagon trains could depart. Sometimes, that took until late May. One by one in the early 1840s, families and wagons and cattle herds began moving west.

Wagon trains coming from Independence first crossed the Blue River. All the caravans moving south of the Missouri River came to "The Line." It was the end of Missouri, and in those days the end of the organized United States. "Once on state line, looking into the Indian territory," writes historian Merrill Mattes, "the country actually looked different."

The land west of the line had been ceded to the Indian tribes in perpetuity. Perpetuity would last only until 1854.

Once in the Indian lands, the wagons headed west and south, past what would become Olathe. By nighttime of the first or second day, wagons and bawling cattle poured into camp. That could be either Lone Elm campground or Elm Grove campground, depending on whether the caravan came from Independence or Westport. The sites are in today's southern Johnson County, Kan., about two miles apart.

"Our long journey," Peter Burnett remembered of the first night of his trip in 1843, "began in sunshine and in song. But all those vanished before we reached its termination."

The next day brought the splitting of the Santa Fe and Oregon trails. Then the Oregon emigrants came to a ford of the Wakarusa River, through an area that would one day become Lawrence, Kan., and on up the road to a group of shanties that would become Topeka.

By that point, the trail had been relatively easy. Many of the emigrants still had high hopes, and were getting along with one another. The feeling would not last.

Mattes was succinct:

"I think if most of them knew what was in store for them they'd never have left Independence."

"ALL WAS HURRY AND CONFUSION AND OFTTIMES THE SHARP TONE OF ANGRY DISPUTE AROSE ABOVE THE JARGON OF THE TUMULTUOUS THRONG…. THE SCENE TO ME PORTRAYED A NOVELTY QUITE AMUSING. I BEGAN TO THINK A MORE COMICAL-LOOKING SET COULD SCARCELY BE FOUND."

— *Rufus B. Sage, 1841*

8 MILES (FROM WESTPORT)

Facing page: *Sapling Grove lay near the road from Westport. The first sizable company of overland emigrants destined for the Pacific coast assembled here in May 1841. Past the Rockies, on the Snake River, the group split, some for Oregon and some for California. Today, the land is part of Comanche Park on Grant Avenue at 82nd Terrace in Overland Park, Kan.*

FREMONT'S EXPEDITION

Explorer John C. Fremont went west in 1842 and again in 1843, plotting the trail to Oregon. Accompanying him was Charles Preuss, who prepared a seven-part map that was ordered published by Congress in 1846. The map of the Oregon trail and of other parts of the West touched the imagination of Americans and spurred emigration. This is the first of seven sections; it shows the trail from Westport in Missouri, into Indian Territory, across the Kansas River and up the Blue River valley until the trail heads northwest to meet the Platte River. Below: the remaining six maps arranged west to east. Fremont's expedition did not go all the way to the Willamette River but stopped where the Walla Walla River met the Columbia. In the enlarged sections in this book, some of Fremont's marginal notes have been removed for space reasons.

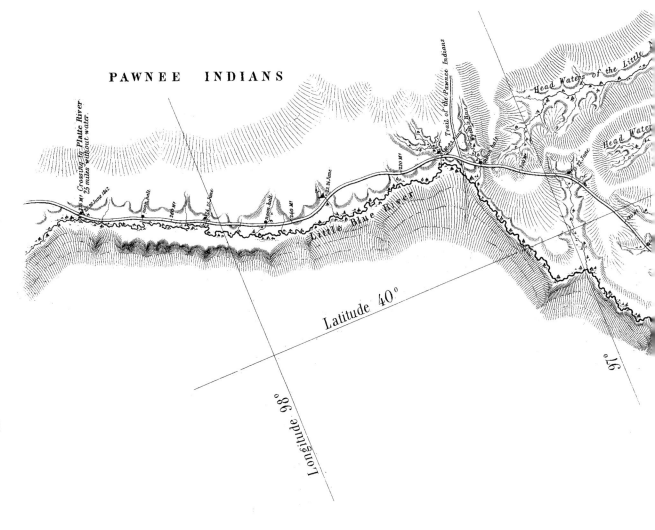

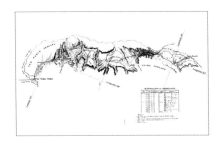

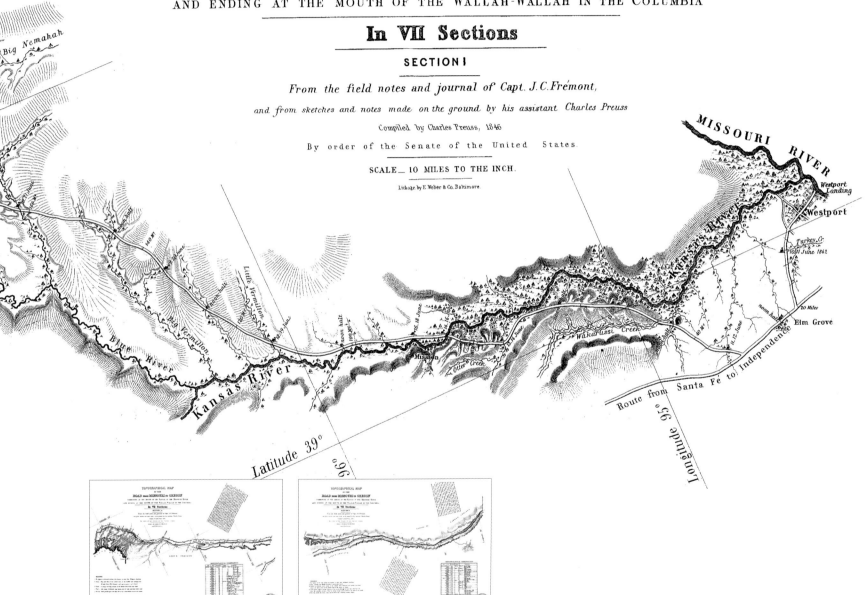

Prairie

Gear

To make wagons durable enough for the long, rocky journey — but not too heavy for animals to pull — strong woods such as hickory, oak, maple and Osage orange were required. Instead of the heavy Conestoga wagons of Pennsylvania, the standard for overland travel was a lighter wagon with straight lines. Iron was used only where strength and durability were most important — for tires, tongue joints and parts of the undercarriage. Wheels were bolted on for easy removal and the rig had to be amphibious for crossing streams. Spare parts, tar buckets, grease barrels, water barrels and rope were standard equipment. The wagon's load could easily exceed a ton, requiring four to six oxen to haul.

Animals

Most of the early emigrants preferred oxen over horses and mules. Two oxen, called a yoke, cost slightly less than a single mule and far less than a single horse. Although slower than horses or mules, oxen were stronger and milder tempered, and also most useful to farmers once they arrived in Oregon.

Expense

Together, wagon and beasts of burden cost the emigrants about $400 — probably equal to $6,000 to $9,000 in today's money.

"ABOUT SUNDOWN WE REACHED A SMALL CREEK KNOWN AS ELM GROVE, AND ENCAMPED FOR THE NIGHT, WITH EVERY INDICATION OF AN APPROACHING STORM....SOME DISPOSED OF THEMSELVES IN, AND OTHERS UNDER, THE WAGONS, MAKING BARRICADES TO THE WINDWARD."

— *Rufus B. Sage, 1841*

30 MILES

Facing page: *At Lone Elm campground, travelers from Independence stopped typically on their second night out. In the 1840s, only a single tree of any size — an elm — stood at the campground, and it eventually was cut down for firewood. This view looks west from the site of the sprawling campground, southeast of today's 167th Street and Lone Elm Road south of Olathe, Kan. Not far northwest of here, on the main route from Westport, was Elm Grove campground. Its site surrounds today's U.S. 56 bridge over Cedar Creek.*

PRAIRIE

"Fine weather. Went about nine miles and dined. Then left the Santa Fe road, traveled about six miles over beautiful prairie and camped on a fine branch of running water, with its banks well wooded with oak, walnut, Linn and ash, timber generally scarce."

– *Virgil Pringle, three days after leaving Independence, May 1846*

40 MILES

Facing page: *Routes from Westport and from Independence carried not only families bound for Oregon and for California, but also traders headed for Santa Fe. The Independence and Westport roads converged briefly west of Lone Elm and Elm Grove campgrounds. Then, well past the Missouri line and into the level prairies, they split again at this point. The lefthand road led southwest to Santa Fe and the other to Oregon and California. This is near present-day Gardner in southern Johnson County, Kan.*

WHY THIS ROUTE?

By the early 1840s, Independence and Westport already were established as outfitting points for commercial caravans to Santa Fe. From these towns it was unnecessary to cross the Missouri River. This made them favorites for early Oregon emigrants. In 1849, St. Joseph began to draw most of the departing emigrants — not only those bound for Oregon but also those headed to the gold fields of California. In the 1850s, towns farther up the Missouri River became primary jumping-off points.

No matter what route was used first, the Platte River Valley served as the main road into the Rocky Mountains. The Platte and its tributary, the Sweetwater River, led to South Pass, which was the easiest way across the Continental Divide. Once over the Rockies, the Snake and Columbia rivers led the emigrants the rest of the way.

PRAIRIE

"HERE WE ARE, MAY 17TH, IN A BEAUTIFUL ENCAMPMENT ON THE (WAKARUSA) RIVER.... LIFE ON THE PRAIRIES FAR SURPASSES MY EXPECTATION; THERE IS A FREEDOM AND A NOBLENESS ABOUT IT THAT TEND TO BRING FORTH THE FULL MANHOOD....TODAY WE HAVE RIPE STRAWBERRIES UPON THE PRAIRIES."

— *George Curry, 1846*

As the Oregon Trail came near this prominence — Blue Mound — it split. Some caravans turned left, moving past the south side of Blue Mound. Travelers often climbed this hill to gain the best view of the countryside since leaving Missouri. This branch of the trail crossed the Wakarusa River upstream a few miles west of here. Other caravans turned right before reaching Blue Mound, fording the Wakarusa and passing well to the north of the hill. The two branches rejoined in what today is downtown Lawrence, Kan.

Sunset at the upstream Wakarusa crossing.

2,000 MILES TO OREGON 15

PRAIRIE

"THE DAY WAS OCCUPIED IN CROSSING THE CREEK — A TASK BY NO MEANS EASY, ITS BANKS BEING SO PRECIPITOUS WE WERE COMPELLED TO LOWER OUR WAGONS BY MEANS OF ROPES. IN SO DOING IT REQUIRED THE UTMOST CAUTION TO PREVENT THEM FROM OVERSETTING OR BECOMING BROKEN IN THE ABRUPT DESCENT."

— *Rufus B. Sage, 1841, on crossing the Wakarusa River.*

TIP FOR THE TRAIL

PROVISIONS (PER PERSON)

~ Flour: 200 pounds
~ Bacon: 150 pounds
~ Coffee: 10 pounds
~ Sugar: 20 pounds
~ Salt: 10 pounds

Emigrants also carried such food items as dried beans, dried fruit, rice, baking soda, vinegar and molasses.

"LET EACH ... BE PROVIDED ... TWO VERY WIDE-BRIMMED HATS, WIDE ENOUGH TO KEEP THE MOUTH FROM THE SUN. FOR THE WANT OF SUCH HAT THOUSANDS SUFFER NEARLY ALL THE WAY TO OREGON, WITH THEIR LIPS ULCERATED, CAUSED BY SUNBURN."

— *J.M. Shively, in his 1846 guide*

55 MILES

Facing page: *Many caravans bound for Oregon crossed the Wakarusa River here and continued northwest. Ruts created as traffic from the south descended the stream's steep banks remain visible at the crossing, which is just south of Kansas 10 east of Lawrence, Kan.*

90 MILES

Oregon emigrants crossed the Kansas River where Topeka would one day rise. By the middle 1840s the main crossing could be made using a ferry operated by two brothers. Before the Gold Rush of 1849 boosted prices, travelers reported the toll was one dollar.

"WE CAME UP THE SOUTH SIDE OF THE KANSAS RIVER AND CAMPED BELOW AND NEAR AN INDIAN TOWN OF THE KANSA TRIBE.... I ADMIRED SEVERAL OF THE INDIAN MEN I SAW THERE. THEY WERE MORE THAN SIX FEET TALL, STRAIGHT, AND MOVED WITH A PROUD STEP....IN CROSSING THE RIVER THE INDIANS ASSISTED OUR PEOPLE IN SWIMMING OUR CATTLE AND HORSES."

– Jesse Applegate, age 7, in 1843.

Prairie

Past the Kansas River, the trail followed country like this, at Riley Creek. Ruts are still in evidence ascending the hill in the distance. The gravel road to the right of them is named Oregon Trail Road. It is in Pottawatomie County, Kan.

Getting organized

It was customary to wait until after crossing the Kansas River — time enough for travelers to become better acquainted — to select permanent leaders of a caravan. Once organized, for several miles the wagons hewed close to the ridge of hills on the north side of the Kansas River valley. Then bending north away from the river, the Oregon Trail crossed an undulating plain.

Prairie

"We traveled 18 miles over a high, rolling prairie, and encamped on the banks of Little Vermillion Creek, in sight of a Kaw village. Our camp here replenished their stores.... These Indians ... conducted themselves honorably in their dealings with us; in view of which we raised for their benefit a contribution of tobacco, lead, &c., and received in return many good wishes for a pleasant and successful journey."

– Joel Palmer, 1845

120 MILES

Facing page: *The steep banks and rapid current of the Little, or Red Vermillion made for a difficult crossing in the 1840s. In 1849, cholera took scores of emigrants' lives at this place and 50 of them were said to have been buried in the area. Three crude stone markers stand on the east bank, one of which is legible: T.S. Prather, May 27, 1849.*

In Years to Come

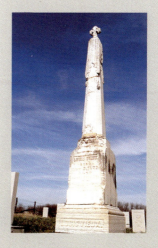

In the 1850s, a toll bridge was built here — at what was called Red Vermillion crossing — by Louis Vieux, a business agent of the Pottawattomie Indians and landowner. His grave marker stands on a hill nearby, northeast of present-day Wamego, Kan.

2,000 Miles to Oregon

PRAIRIE

145 MILES

Now heading almost due north through the watershed of the Big Blue River, the Oregon Trail coursed over this rolling prairie, left.

Below: The ruts descending this hill today appear as a smooth depression extending from upper right to lower left in this photograph. The scene is south of where Cricket Road meets Parallel Road today, at the Pottawatomie-Marshall County line in Kansas.

DEATH

Above: *The gravestone of T.S. Prather, who died in 1849 and is buried at the Little, or Red Vermillion crossing. Today, a chainlink fence erected at the grave casts a shadow on the inscription.* Below: *Rachel Pattison died the same year, hundreds of miles up the trail near Ash Hollow, in what is now Nebraska. Probably both were victims of cholera.*

The trail took its toll in human life — 30,000 in two decades — one man, woman or child for every 193 yards of the road west. Cholera got a lot of them. Also, there were measles, dysentery, mumps, scarlet fever, typhoid and smallpox. Children died after they were run over by heavy wagons. Barely one in 100 died in battles with Indians.

"Passed seven new man-made graves," Cecelia Adams wrote in her diary in 1852. "One had four bodies in it … cholera. A man died with the cholera ahead of us."

With dreadful monotony, her list grew longer as the trail grew shorter.

"Another man died….Passed six new graves….We have passed 21 new man-made graves….Made 18 miles. Passed 13 graves today….Passed 10 graves."

Today, most of those graves are lost, and it is hardly surprising. Most graves were shallow to save labor, so bodies were washed away or dragged away by animals. Suitable headstones that could withstand weather and time were rare.

Sarah Keyes wasn't even trying to make it all the way to California. She was blind, deaf and may have suffered consumption. But the 70-year-old woman hoped only to reach Fort Hall on the Snake River in the summer of 1846. There she could meet her only son, an earlier emigrant to Oregon, for one last reunion. She got no farther than Alcove Spring on the Blue River.

Today, Sarah Keyes' gravestone is gone. Where she lies no one knows.

"Mr. Collins' son George, about 6 years old, fell from the wagon and the wheels ran over his head, killing him instantly; the remainder of the day occupied in burying him at the place where leave the river."

– Virgil Pringle on the Bear River, 1846

165 MILES

Named by travelers who eventually turned off this trail and headed to California, Alcove Spring was a font of cool, clear water. This waterfall is its most scenic feature. The creek branch created by the spring flows into the Blue River close to a ford used by trail travelers. As for the group bound for California, it was part of the ill-fated 1846 Donner Party. Just east of the spring today, U.S. 77 connects Blue Rapids and Marysville, Kan.

IN YEARS TO COME

In 1858 this commercial supply store, Hollenberg Station, was built along the Oregon Trail. The original portion in the center was expanded in 1860. Today, it is a Kansas State Historic Site east of Hanover, Kan.

2,000 MILES TO OREGON

200 MILES

Wagon wheels dug deep into the prairie where the Oregon Trail crossed Rock Creek. Today this is in Jefferson County, in southeast Nebraska.

Prairie

In Years to Come

In 1857, a decade and a half after the first substantial migration along the Oregon Trail, a ranch and store were established at Rock Creek. These sold supplies not only to emigrants but also to stage and freight lines that used the road through what had become Nebraska Territory. Today, the buildings used by that operation have been reconstructed and are part of Rock Creek Station State Historical Park east of Fairbury, Neb.

A Legend is Born

James Butler Hickok was a 24-year-old employee of the Overland Stage Co. in 1861 when he was assigned to duty at Rock Creek Station. His company, which was buying part of the ranch, fell behind on its payments and former ranch owner David McCanles attempted to collect. Possibly Hickok shot McCanles and two of his hired men, but no one knows for sure or why. What is for sure is that the tale, much glamorized in Hickok's favor, appeared in February 1867 in *Harper's*. Supposedly, Hickok single-handedly fought 10 men in the "M'Kandlas' gang" and despite severe wounds beat them all. "Wild Bill" Hickok was suddenly a star.

High Plains

The Oregon Trail from Missouri met the Platte River near the bottom of the river's long, southward loop across the Plains.

There, more than a century and a half ago, overland emigrants first saw the stream that would lead them to the Rockies and almost halfway to their goal — Oregon.

"From the sandhills," James Evans wrote in 1850, "it had the appearance of a great inland sea. It looked wider than the Mississippi…. There is no tree timber here growing on the margin of the river, not even a willow switch."

A few emigrants called what they saw the "Coast of Nebraska." The word Nebraska was Indian; the English equivalent was "flat water."

"The vast shimmering flatness … did have a remarkable resemblance to the seashore of the Atlantic Ocean," wrote Merrill J. Mattes, the historian of the Platte River road. "It was

"WE SET OUT AT THE USUAL HOUR AND CROSSED OVER THE COUNTRY TO PLATTE RIVER…. NEAR US THE PLATTE BOTTOM IS THREE AND A HALF MILES WIDE, COVERED WITH EXCELLENT GRASS, WHICH OUR CATTLE ATE GREEDILY….IN THE EVENING IT RAINED VERY HARD."

— Joel Palmer, 1845

The Platte River today is only a fraction of its 1840s width. This portion is near North Platte, Neb.

28   2,000 MILES TO OREGON

High Plains

prophetic that this first exposure to the Platte produced an eerie, unearthly (or at least unfamiliar) atmosphere that created an aura for the remaining journey."

In 1832, Army Capt. Benjamin E. Bonneville measured the river at 2,200 yards from bank to bank.

To the emigrants, the river was a wild, living thing. They would remember how the wide Platte looked like a loose braid, tendrils of water amid sandbars. At sunset the water would turn silver, then gold.

> "Every night we encamped, we locate quite a village but take it up the next day. We have plenty of music with the flute and violin and some dancing."
>
> – Elizabeth Dixon Smith, 1847

"The river is over a mile wide … with a current outrunning the Missouri … and its course over an uneven bottom, boiling and eddying until it completely mixed with sand," said James Bennett.

They would remember the crossings, either ridiculously easy in dry spells or terrifying in wet ones.

"Into this flood, fearful and dangerous to look at, our wagons commenced plunging one after another … ," Bennett said of the crossing of the South Platte above where it joined the North. "On reaching the opposite shore the drivers found the legs of the pantaloons literally cut to pieces by the sand and force of

The great road

"One of the best natural roads, of the distance of 400 miles, that is to be found on the face of the earth," said one traveler about the trail beside the Platte River, as quoted by historian Merrill J. Mattes. The route was just right for emigration because it was dry, level and it ran in the right direction — namely, toward the most easily accessible opening through the Rocky Mountains, South Pass. This natural highway across the High Plains featured few trees — only a few cottonwoods and willows on islands in the stream — and grama, galleta and buffalo grass. To build fires, emigrants used dry buffalo dung, or buffalo chips; buffalo were still plentiful in the 1840s, as were antelopes.

> "We see thousands of buffalo and have to use their dung for fuel. A man will gather a bushel in a minute. Three bushels makes a good fire."
>
> – Elizabeth Dixon Smith, 1847

High Plains

the water."

At night after the crossings, the wagons would gather in a circle; the horses and mules would be tethered inside. The cattle would graze outside the circle. The men would repair the wagons and tend to their animals. Women would seek out buffalo chips for fuel to cook fires; even a piece of driftwood was rare on this river. And eventually the circle would settle down. There would be quiet talk, maybe about the crossing, maybe the descent of Windlass Hill coming up, maybe about the strange rock formations that the guides said loomed ahead.

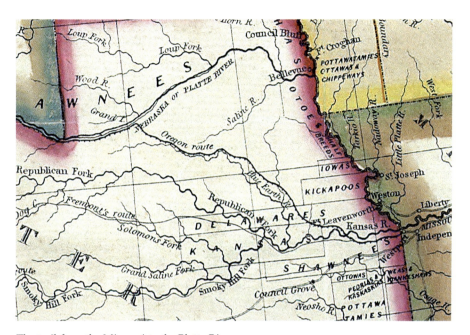

The trail from the Missouri to the Platte River.

310 MILES

Fort Kearny

To protect emigrants, this military post was established next to the Platte River in 1848, and named after Stephen Watts Kearny, a hero of the Mexican War. Its first structures were made of adobe and timber, and its business did not take off until the Gold Rush.

STORMS

In wet weather, emigrants fought mud, in dry weather dust. Much of the time strong winds blew. But nothing was comparable to the thunderstorms that swept across the Plains and down on the caravans. They brought fierce lightning, deafening thunder, and hard rain. Occasionally hail and tornadoes kicked in.

"THE RAIN CAME DOWN IN BUCKETFULS, DRENCHING US TO THE SKIN. THERE WASN'T A TENT IN THE CAMP THAT HELD AGAINST THE TERRIFIC WIND. THE MEN HAD TO CHAIN THE WAGONS TOGETHER TO KEEP THEM FROM BEING BLOWN IN THE RIVER."

— Mary Elizabeth Munkers Estes, 10 years old when her family was on the trail for Oregon in 1846.

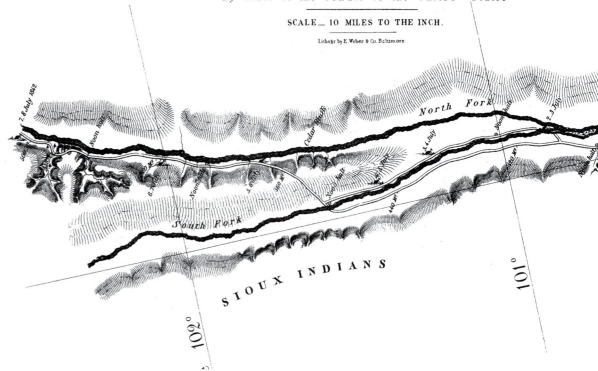

485 MILES

Crossing

When the caravans arrived at the two forks that joined to form the Platte River, they had to continue along the northernmost to reach Fort Laramie. That required crossing the south fork, or South Platte. This section of the Fremont map shows one such crossing. Jessy Quinn Thornton crossed in June 1846: "The river here was about a mile and a half wide . … (It) had a quicksand bottom and it was necessary therefore to avoid stopping the teams in the river, because … the wagons immediately commenced sinking."

Then the travelers trudged up to the plateau between the river forks, only to descend sharply after about 15 more miles into Ash Hollow, a four-mile plain extending to the North Platte. It contained an excellent spring.

PLODDING ALONG

"They will quarrel ... till the company will divide and subdivide, the whole way to Oregon.... Let no one leave dependent on his best friend for any thing; for if you do, you will certainly have a blow-out before you get far."

— *J.M. Shively's guide, 1846.*

"Strong sentiments of mutiny.... some want to cross the river here, some want to go ahead, and others want to go any way but the right way."

— *James Nesmith, 1843*

On a July day in the 1840s, along the North Platte River valley, 500-plus miles and eight weeks from the Missouri River, these things could have been seen from afar:

Tiny canvas-topped wagons pulled mostly by oxen, not in one long line but in small groups — some abreast of each other, some trailing slightly to the rear, others far off to the side. And more: tiny figures driving the wagons; others trudging beside them; still others riding or walking behind the rearguard cattle herd.

Most filthy. Some of the children barefoot. And all — the people, the livestock and the wagons — moving at not much more than a snail's pace — two, maybe three miles an hour as they trudged across the land along the river.

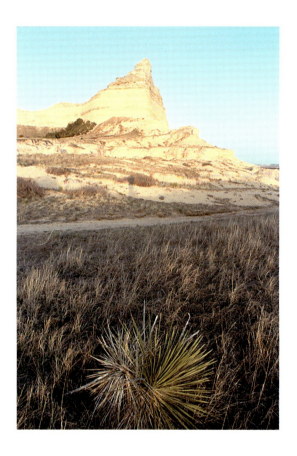

One other thing: dust. Gritty, gray-brown dust that, once disturbed by hooves, iron-rimmed wagon wheels and worn boots, rose like a fog, leading one journal-keeper to refer to these as "smoky" days. And when the wind blew, the dust felt like tiny bird shot.

Still two weeks from Fort Laramie, the dancing chimera of Oregon had faded, pushed aside by more practical matters — organization of the train, the need to be continually on the move and the conflicting personalities of the emigrants.

Old journals and diaries reveal that the emigrants, like modern counterparts with a new car, had finally figured out how best to operate the conveyances they were tied to for the long trip. That meant what kind of load the oxen could pull without losing weight as the grass became thinner along the trail, how much had to be off-loaded before a river crossing, when a squeaking wheel was truly in need of grease.

And more. The "cow column" was banished to the rear because of the dust several thousand cattle raised. Trains were headed by wagons belonging to families with fewer than three cows each. That group was broken down even further — into platoons of fours so that every fourth day a different wagon would be in the lead and not eat dust as the platoons spread out across the prairie.

Ahead of everybody was a guide who each day led a handful of men ahead of the wagons, marking the trail, flagging creek crossings and boggy spots, picking locations for the nightly camp, making sure enough wood, grass and water was available.

The arrangements, naturally, didn't suit everyone.

Some complained. Some got in enough of a snit to leave the main columns, traveling a few miles away from the main group.

Some — called "turnbackers" — already had left the trains, fed up with the rains that had made for difficult crossings, the choking dust, the nighttime guard duty, the daily chores. In later years, disease and death forced some back.

Jesse Applegate, who made the trek in 1843, remembered years afterward:

"The (emigrants) were probably brave enough but would never submit to discipline as soldiers. If the President had started across the plains … the first time he should choose a bad camp or in any way offend them, they would turn him out."

J. Goldsborough Bruff, who crossed in 1849, found that by July, "all bad traits of the men now well developed, — their true character is shown, untrammeled, unvarnished. Selfishness, hypocrisy, &c. Some whom at home were thought gentlemen are now totally unprincipled."

The shortage of camaraderie would lead to some bizarre occurrences. Six years after the 1843 train, wrote Merrill Mattes, "two

Plodding Along

quarrelsome emigrants sawed their wagon in half and flipped for the front end!"

Apparently, the front of the wagon made a better cart to continue the journey.

Through this part of Indian Territory — it would become Nebraska Territory in 1854 — the columns made good time. It was drier, the grass was adequate and the occasional stream was less a barrier than had been the Kansas or the Platte.

Ahead on the trail was Fort Laramie, then a trading post for the mountain men whose way of life had faded. By the 1840s it was a market for the Indian harvest of buffalo robes.

For the emigrants, the fort would offer the first taste of civilization in two months. So they didn't delay as they moved across the flat plains that steadily rose westward. But while keeping up the pace, they did a very human thing: They became tourists.

Along the trail were huge, weirdly shaped, almost surreal rock formations unlike anything most of those in the train had ever seen.

Landmarks such as Courthouse and Jail Rocks, Chimney Rock, and, finally, the massive

> "SAW CHIMNEY ROCK. IT IS A CURIOSITY INDEED. ALL OF THE LOFTY ROCKS ALONG HERE ARE COMPOSED OF THE SAME MATERIAL. SOME OF THEM RESEMBLE OLD DEMOLISHED VILLAGES HALF STUCK IN THE GROUND WITH STOVEPIPES STICKING OUT AT THE TOP."
>
> *Elizabeth Dixon Smith, 1847*

575 MILES

Emigrants marveled at Chimney Rock, among the first of several natural landmarks they met along the North Platte. In 1841 Rufus Sage called it "an extraordinary curiosity that had continued in view and excited our admiration....truly — a wonderful display of the eccentricity of Nature!" Today U.S. 26 runs past it in Morrill County in the Nebraska panhandle.

Plodding Along

595 MILES

Scotts Bluff reminded travelers of another realm.

"There are here several ranges of detached Sand Hills, running parallel with the river, the sides of which are almost perpendicular, destitute of vegetation, and so washed by the rains of thousands of years, as to present, at a distance, the appearance of Cities, Temples, Castles, Towers, Palaces, and every variety of great and magnificent structures," wrote Overton Johnson, who traveled the trail in 1843.

Richard Burton, an English traveler, rhapsodized about his view of Courthouse Rock: "I saw it when set off by weather to advantage. A blazing sun rained fire upon its cream coloured surface … and it stood boldly out against a purple-black nimbus which overspread the southern skies, growling distant thunders, and flashing red threads of chained lightning."

Preceding pages: Scott's Bluff, a sandstone formation similar to Chimney Rock, evidently was named for a fur trader named Scott who died nearby after being abandoned by his companions. Scores of versions of the story differ on how long he was abandoned, how he died and so on.
Right: Trail ruts at Scott's Bluff National Monument.

The land truly was different.

Something else had happened, too. Now what looked like a mile away actually was five. There was a shimmering quality to the atmosphere and panorama the emigrants beheld. This was the West.

Yet they didn't tarry. Ahead was Fort Laramie. And beyond that was a trace heading northwest, then back southwest and onward to the fabled South Pass through the Rocky Mountains, the path to what one later diarist called "the other side of the world."

40   2,000 MILES TO OREGON

The long road

The maps prepared from John C. Fremont's expedition show the long, straight route along the Platte River marked by the Chimney Rock and Scott's Bluff outcroppings.

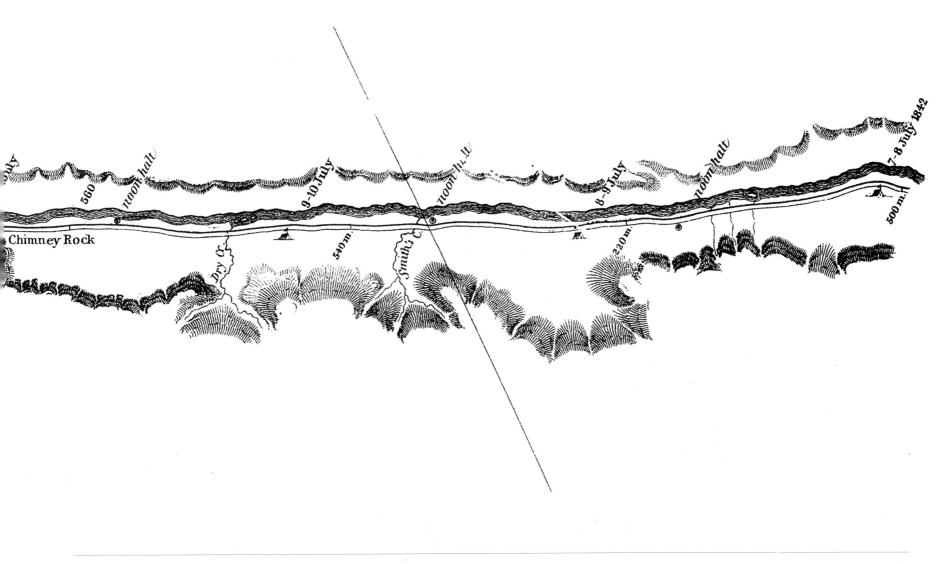

FORT LARAMIE

650 MILES

"FORT JOHN, OR LARAMIE ... IS ON THE LEFT BANK, ON A RISING GROUND SOME TWENTY-FIVE FEET ABOVE THE WATER; AND ITS LOFTY WALLS, WHITEWASHED AND PICKETED, WITH THE LARGE BASTIONS AT THE ANGLES, GAVE IT QUITE AN IMPOSING APPEARANCE."

— *John C. Fremont, 1842*

Facing page: *Originally named Fort William and then Fort John, but typically known as Fort Laramie, a trading post stood since 1834 near the Laramie River's entry into the Platte. In 1849 it was taken over by the U.S. military. These ruins date from 1873; they are of the post hospital.*

Fort Laramie was the first major stop on the Oregon Trail, and it was vital to those going on through the mountains. It was a place to fix wagons, shoe sore-footed oxen and mules, trade cattle for fresh livestock, and, above all, to reprovision at the store.

"Like locusts, they fell on the storerooms of Fort Laramie, ... driving prices up with their own competition and then complaining of high costs," historian David Lavender wrote about the first large caravan over the trail in 1843.

Such prices (sugar was $2 a cup; tobacco, 5 cents back in the states, went for $1.50) would stick in the craw (and appear in the diaries) of overlanders from that year on.

Yet the travelers were learning to make do with less. Diary after diary remarks on the abandonment of less-needed supplies as loads were lightened for the steepening road ahead.

'The abandonment and destruction of property here is extraordinary," John Goldsborough Bruff observed on July 17, 1849. "A great deal is heavy, cumbrous, useless articles; a diving bell and all the apparatus, heavy anvils, iron and steel, forges, bellows, lead & c. and provisions — bacon in great piles."

Other visitors were simply disappointed in Fort Laramie, which they had hoped would be a last bit of civilization before moving on into the Rockies.

"My glowing fancy vanished before the wretched reality," William Kelly wrote about Laramie in 1849, the year the U.S. Army bought the post and turned it into a fort. Kelly described "a miserable, cracked, dilapidated, adobe, quadrangular enclosure."

The nearby river and the fort were named after Jacque LaRamee, a French trapper. The first structure on the site, a cottonwood log stockade, apparently was called Fort William, named after William Sublette. He and Jim

Fort Laramie

660 MILES

Bridger were owners for a while, selling the place to the American Fur Co. By 1841, an adobe structure rose on the site. The name was changed to Fort John, after a company director in St. Louis, but it soon became known as Fort Laramie.

It was the American Fur Co. that saw the new market in the shape of those first foot-sore emigrants, tired livestock and worn wagons.

Not a big market immediately, according to Le Roy Hafen and Francis M. Young, chroniclers of the old fort. That wouldn't come until 1850 and the California gold fever that gripped the trail and the nation, and mobs of people poured west. In that year, on the single day of Aug. 14, 39,506 people and 9,927 wagons passed through Fort Laramie.

Just west of Fort Laramie, wagons carved these deep ruts in the sandstone. They are on Deep Rut Hill near Guernsey, Wyo.

Meanwhile, furs remained important in the post's business. And that fur was buffalo — robes for fireplace rugs and to warm those on carriage rides. The furs were brought to Fort Laramie by Indians.

E. Douglas Branch in *The Hunting of the Buffalo* wrote that perhaps 20,000 robes a year were shipped east during the 1840s.

Indians would came to Fort Laramie to trade, pick up government annuities and see

the emigrants.

"I remember with what terror I saw the Indians come out from Ft. Laramie. They looked so naked and wild," said 11-year-old Lucy Ann Henderson Deady in 1846. "The men got out their guns, but all the Indians wanted was to see us and to see if we would give them anything."

Fort Laramie represented the coming destruction of the buffalo and the eventual disappearance of ways of life for an entire culture of nomadic people.

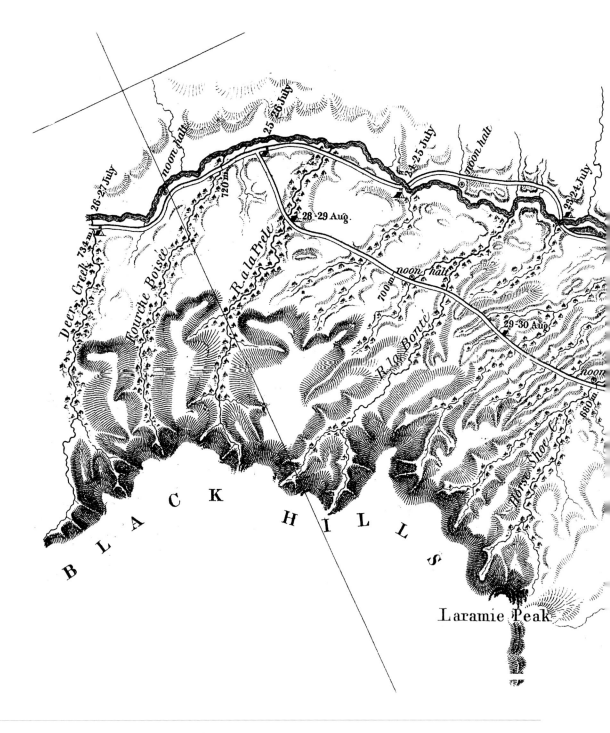

Right: *A section of the 1846 Fremont map.*

THE ROCKY MOUNTAINS

Caravans encountered this region, a mix of mountains, plateaus and valleys, west of Fort Laramie as they ascended first the North Platte and then the valley of its tributary, the Sweetwater River. On the way to South Pass, the caravans crossed the Black Hills (called the Laramie Mountains today) and then the Rockies proper. Now the route was marked by frequent ascents and descents, which tired out emigrants and animals and which wore on wagons. Along the North Platte, forage and water were adequate; the Sweetwater valley brought drier conditions and less vegetation. Days were hot; nights were cold.

INDEPENDENCE ROCK

"On the third day of July, we encamped in the shadow of Independence Rock....The next day being the 4th of July we concluded to lay by and celebrate the day. The children had no fireworks, but we all joined in singing patriotic songs and shared in a picnic lunch. Some spent considerable time carving their names on the great rock. This seemed to be the rule of all emigrants passing that way."

– *Margaret M. Hecox, 1846*

For the emigrant, no place was better for celebrating the Fourth of July than this. Besides the patriotic significance of the name, they knew that reaching Independence Rock by Independence Day meant they should beat the snows of the farthest mountains.

So it was here the satisfied overlanders circled their wagons, watered their stock in the Sweetwater River and got out their diaries.

"Huge whale," "bowl," "sway-backed hummock," "globe," "half hump," "turtle-shaped," "clear granite," and "huge monster rising from the ground" were some of the descriptions they offered.

People have been coming and meeting here for ages. First were the Indians who developed

815 MILES

Independence Rock, first of a wave of landmarks lining the Oregon Trail in the Sweetwater River valley.

Independence Rock

intricate legends about the igneous formation of feldspar and mica. Then came Robert Stuart in 1812, the Britisher credited with the discovery of South Pass, the key to the Oregon Trail. His journal indicated he camped near Independence Rock on Oct. 30, 1812, although he made no mention of the actual rock.

"Probably," says trail historian Gregory Franzwa, "Stuart thought, after all he's been through, that it was just another big rock."

The naming of the rock apparently occurred July 4, 1830, and is attributed by the Wyoming Historical Society to William Sublette, the trader.

Trappers, emigrants, traders and just about everybody else who passed this way — meaning just about all the hundreds of thousands who used the trail to reach Oregon, California or Utah — saw, stopped, walked around and marveled at the rock.

It might seem that most either carved, painted or used a mixture of grease and gunpowder to inscribe their names (or the names of those who already had died along the trail). Diaries recorded that enterprising Mormons set up shop at the rock and did the carving for $1 to $5 a name. Among those names was that of the Rev. Pierre-Jean DeSmet, the Jesuit who ranged all over the West in that era. In the early 1840s, DeSmet wrote:

"The famous rock Independence, which is detached, like an outwork, from the immense chain of mountains that divide North America; it has been designated the Backbone of the world; it might also be called the great registry of the desert; for on it may be read in large characters the names of the several travelers who have visited the Rocky Mountains.

"My name figures among so many others as that of the first priest who has visited these solitary regions."

Many of the other marks are gone, the painted ones scoured off by weather, the carved ones only barely visible because granite exfoliates or scales itself.

19th-century graffiti atop Independence Rock

Independence Rock

Historian Howard R. Driggs writes that the landmark was mentioned in practically all the trail diaries. He noted one by Wilford Woodruff, who stayed with a group of Missouri emigrants one night and then climbed to the 193-foot summit.

"On the highest point," wrote Driggs, "they offered up their morning prayers.… While they were engaged in these devotions, the Missourians were burying one of their number, Rachel Morgan, a woman of twenty-five years, near the rock. She was the third of her family to pass away on this hard journey."

Such simple incidents defined Independence Rock in the memories of the wayfarers, Driggs wrote.

"Many a wedding was performed there. Social gatherings around the campfire were not infrequent. The old pile often echoed with the music of the fiddle, the accordion, and the banjo while travelers joined in the dance."

Modern path at Independence Rock State Historic Site, off Wyoming Highway 220 in Natrona County, Wyo. southwest of Casper.

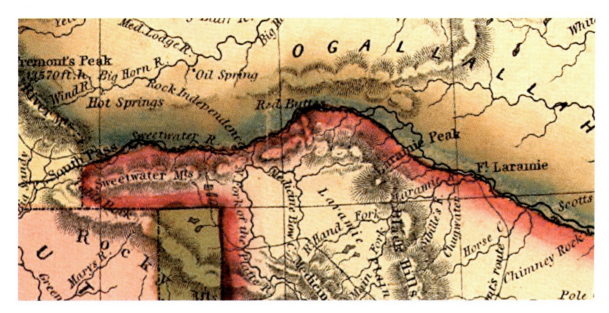
Augustus Mitchell's map of 1846: From Ft. Laramie to the Continental Divide.

Toward the Divide

"A short distance from Independence Rock was the Devil's Gate where Sweetwater had worn its way through…. Looking overhead it looked like we might jump from one wall to the other, it was so narrow at the top."

— *J.M. Harrison, 1846*

As the Oregon Trail ascended the eastern slope of the Rocky Mountains, it followed the Sweetwater River, through a valley filled with geological mileposts. Shortly after Independence Rock came Devil's Gate, followed by Split Rock, a cleft in a mountain, then the Castle Rock formation, Ice Slough and so on.

The narrow Devil's Gate, cut by the Sweetwater River, was noted in many journals.

"Some of the boys clambered up the rocks on the N. Side of the Gate, and reached some cavernous places, where they fired pistols and threw down rocks, pleased with the reverberation, which was great," remarked J. Goldsborough Bruff on July 26, 1849.

840 MILES

The landmarks continue: Split Rock.

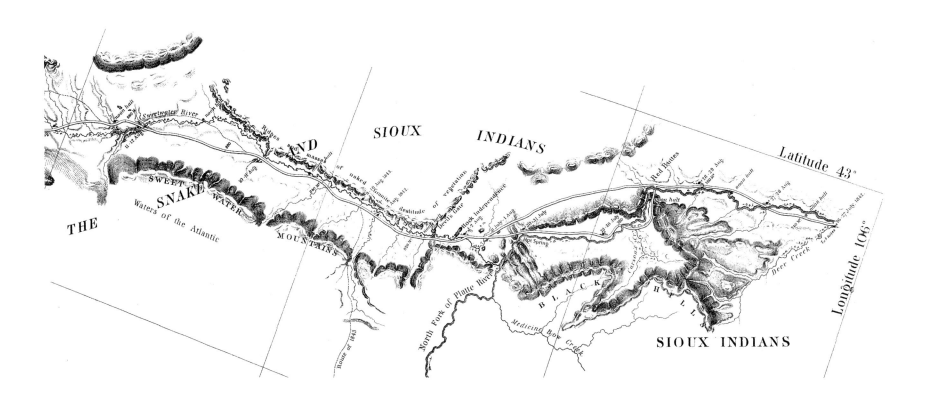

"RIDGES AND MASSES OF NAKED GRANITE DESTITUTE OF VEGETATION."

— Fremont description of the Sweetwater River valley.

Toward the Divide

Naturally, an emigrant fell off occasionally.

Nevertheless, this was a relatively easy part of the trail. Disease had largely abated by this time, the dust wasn't so bad and the treacherous crossings of the North Platte were well behind them.

Warned by their guides, the overlanders would drive — club sometimes — their livestock past the alkali water holes around the Red Buttes, just west of what is now Casper.

By that point, most wagon trains had covered more than 800 miles in about 12 weeks. People were tired and stock was thin from the sparse grass that grew around the base of the sagebrush.

The wagons — repaired at Fort Laramie after nearly being shaken apart on the washboard of countless buffalo ruts — were beginning to show signs of wear again. More cargo was being jettisoned; the hardest grades were still ahead.

Generations later, ranchers and work crews would find an old prairie schooner buried in the sandy soil, cache after cache of goods buried in out-of-the-way places and containing items from soap to old letters, condiments to clothing.

Despite those sacrifices, a palpable excitement had been building.

The land was rising toward the Continental Divide; the air was imperceptibly thinning, and the nights were getting cooler, leaving frost on the sagebrush and a scum of ice in the kettles and buckets.

Wrote James Bennett on July 16, 1850: "Since we arrived on the Sweetwater, the nights have been cool, with slight frosts. A clear moonlight night followed a warm and sultry day and as we clustered around our campfire, the fatigues, hardships and perplexities of the journey were in a measure forgotten."

But for William Newby, a member of the 1843 wagon train, "It is cool enough of nites for a man to set in a stove room with an over cote on."

Just ahead was the magical South Pass. Once through it, the emigrants would finally have left Indian Territory, which they had crossed into only a day or two after beginning their journey. Now they entered Oregon Territory, which extended west from the Rockies to the Pacific Ocean. Granted, it was still a long way from the Continental Divide to the Willamette Valley. But the emigrants could say they were halfway there.

So they had some good things to say about South Pass: Charles Stanton gushed on July 19, 1846: "The green meadow land, stretching in some instances as far as the eye could reach in and around them, still heightening the charm of this unequalled scenery."

The Oregon wagon trains kept moving. Settlement of this region, which would eventually become Wyoming, wouldn't come until the 1870s and 1880s, when a few hardy souls decided that with luck and enough rain, cattle and sheep might grow amid the sagebrush, and an alfalfa crop might be wrested from the land along the river.

South Pass

> "The great daydream of my youth and of my riper years is accomplished. I have seen the Rocky Mountains — have crossed the Rubicon and am now on the waters that flow to the Pacific! It seems as if I had left the old world behind and that a new one is dawning upon me."
>
> — Charles Stanton, July 19, 1846.

At South Pass, travelers reached the backbone of North America, as they liked to call the Continental Divide.

A powerful moment. Not only was South Pass the halfway point for their seemingly endless ox-powered trek, but it was where the emigrant left the United States behind. So, what were they thinking now?

"We now consider ourselves in the Oregon territory," wrote Jim Nesmith in his diary, "and we consider this part a poor sample of El Dorado."

Theodore Talbot took the same tack: " 'The land of promise' as yet only promises an increased supply of wormwood and sand."

Indeed, the pass was a bit anticlimactic.

In reality, this 29-mile-wide saddle between the Wind River Mountains on the north and the Antelope Hills on the south is only a long, wide and gently sloping valley. One side barely tilts east toward the Atlantic Ocean, the other side drops a little faster to the Pacific.

"Had we not been told," Overton Johnson wrote, "we should have passed over the dividing ridge through the grand pass of the Rocky Mountains without knowing it."

William Newby, not one of the better spellers on the trail, remarked: "The mane mountain is a graduel desente up & allso the same down. If you dident now it was the mountain you woldent now it from aney outher … "

Some pioneers actually did miss going over the hump. The traveler today could do

915 MILES

Facing page: South Pass, 29 miles wide and only 7,550 feet above sea level, provided the easiest route through the formidable Rocky Mountains.

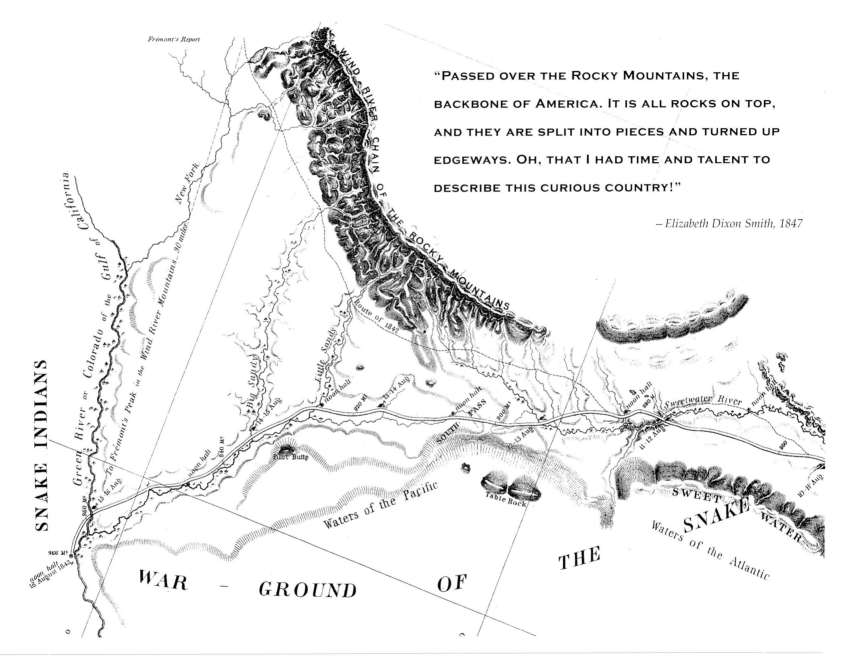

"Passed over the Rocky Mountains, the backbone of America. It is all rocks on top, and they are split into pieces and turned up edgeways. Oh, that I had time and talent to describe this curious country!"

– Elizabeth Dixon Smith, 1847

South Pass

The Climate

John C. Fremont kept extensive climate records on his trek west. On the six days surrounding his crossing of South Pass in August 1846, he recorded mid-day temperatures ranging from the low 60s to the mid-80s. Sunrise lows ranged from the high 20s to the low 40s. Six years later, Henry Page wrote: "The air is cool and bracing and much like the last of the Indian summer which we have in the states. The nights are cool but still dry and healthy. Last night I was on guard and slept part of the night rolled in a buffalo robe, without inconvenience."

Preceding page: South Pass — so gradual that emigrants barely knew when they crossed the Continental Divide.

the same.

Yet its very lack of grandeur was what made the Oregon emigration possible, along with the California and Mormon trails. The pass used by the Lewis and Clark expedition was far to the north, and far too difficult for wagon traffic.

The existence of South Pass became known to Americans as the result of an expedition chartered in 1810 by John Jacob Astor, who was seeking ways to transport furs to the mouth of the Columbia River. His overland explorers came to a dead end trying to navigate the Snake River, and sent parties back east for help. Robert Stuart, heading up a team, came upon the wide, gently sloping South Pass.

When mountain men Jim Bridger, James Clyman, Jedediah Smith and Jim Beckwourth went over South Pass in 1824, they recognized its importance. John C. Fremont, reconnoitering the area in 1842, did, too. He likened the grade to "the ascent of the Capitol Hill" back in Washington.

After more than 800 miles and 80 days on the trail, lashed by rain, choked with dust, remembering steep hills and steep-banked streams, the emigrants could appreciate this gentle grade.

Ahead would be far more difficult climbs — the Blue Mountains and, for those who came after 1846, the infamous Barlow Road around Mount Hood.

"My trip was pleasant until I got to the South Pass — after that the country was rugged and bad roads," recalled a disillusioned Hezekiah Packingham in 1847.

But ultimately, this place was more than just a place.

"I stood or rather stopped my horses on the highest place or culminating point & gave a farewell to the East & thought of the associations that cluster around the words 'sweet home,' " wrote Peter Decker on June 16, 1849.

Lucy Rutledge Cooke had a more succinct way of putting it: "We are now on the other side of the world."

South Pass

In Years to Come

Born in a gold fever that swept this area in the late 1860s, South Pass City soon boasted more than 1,000 residents, along with stores, hotels and saloons. By 1872 the gold boom had turned to bust and ranching became the dominant occupation. Today 24 buildings of the boom era remain. The historic site is on a gravel road off Wyoming Highway 28.

Cutoff — or Not?

> "By taking this trail two and a half days' travel may be saved; but in the forty miles between Big Sandy and Green rivere there is no water, and but little grass."
>
> — *Joel Palmer, 1845*

At the legendary Sublette Cutoff near the south-flowing Big Sandy River, emigrants more than a century and a half ago faced a hard choice.

They could turn southward on the established route, down the Big Sandy to the Green River and then along Black's Fork of the Green to Fort Bridger. There the mountain man Jim Bridger and his partner, Louis Vasquez, had established a post in 1843. Then, the trail took them back north.

The other choice for the emigrants, their oxen and wagons was to go straight ahead, westward into the fearful Little Colorado Desert, miles and miles with choking dust, little grass, and absolutely no water to be found for

930 MILES

Wide open and waterless: The Sublette Cutoff

Cutoff — or Not?

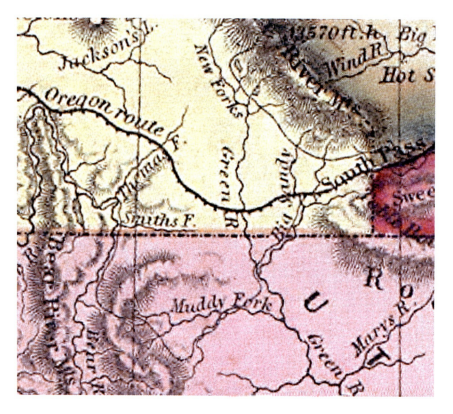

Augustus Mitchell's map of 1846 showed the Sublette Cutoff as the primary route on the road to Oregon. A thin line traces the way south, past Fort Bridger, which is not marked on this map.

the teams over at least two days.

Longer and safer, or quicker and more dangerous?

The first big train of 1843 did go down the Sandy to Fort Bridger, found hardly any supplies on hand, then turned back northwest, heading for the Bear River valley and Idaho.

And starting in 1847, many of the 70,000 Mormons coming from the east passed through the post, bound for Utah.

Jim Bridger expected some traffic in Indian furs when he set up the little fort ("a miserable pen," as one gold seeker described it). But clearly Bridger expected the big profit would come from the overlanders.

"I have established a small fort with a blacksmith shop and a supply of iron in the road of the emigrants ... which promises fairly," the old trapper said in a letter dictated to the Chouteaus in St. Louis. "They, in coming out, are generally well supplied with money...."

Some emigrants considered the fort's prices outrageous. A pint of liquor was $2, as high a

Cutoff — or Not?

price as found anywhere on the trail. Cash or cattle and nothing else was demanded as payment.

Back up the trail was the fork later called the Parting of the Ways. Here about a third of the Oregon-bound emigrants made their decision and went straight ahead into the desert. The cutoff joined the trail again miles to the west.

Daunting as it appeared, Sublette's Cutoff (earlier known as Greenwood's) offered a bonus — speed.

That became more and more important for the emigrants as the years went by. The

> "THIS DAY, WE TRAVELED ABOUT 16 MILES, CROSSED THE CREEK SEVERAL TIMES, AND ENCAMPED NEAR FORT BRIDGER. THIS IS A TRADING FORT.... IT IS BUILT OF POLES AND DAUBED WITH MUD; IT IS A SHABBY CONCERN."
>
> — Joel Palmer, 1845

The barren Sublette Cutoff.

Cutoff — or Not?

average trip from the Missouri River to Oregon took 169 days in the years from 1841 to 1848. That figure dropped to 129 days by 1849.

Part of the savings came from subsequent caravans learning from the experiences of the earlier trains and more ferries established to speed up crossings. The later Oregon wagons might have been hurried along by the anxious 49ers in the caravans, as well as the general shift from oxen to faster mules.

"The slow pace of an ox team is enough to weary anyone's patience, especially those whose palms are itching for gold," commented James Wilkins in 1849.

The overlanders usually reached the cutoff in mid-August, a season of 90-plus-degree heat, no rain, and billowing dust. They weren't dumb. They headed across at night. Often the wagons went 12 abreast. The tracks of those phalanxes are still visible.

The cutoff made an impression on those who crossed it. This is from the 1849 journal of J. Goldsborough Bruff:

"Aug. 4. — Having filled up our water kegs and canteens, at 4 p.m., we left for the long drive, various estimated, from 35 to 55 ms. without water, and only in one spot a little grass … the greater portion of the route level and good.

"Also, that by the way of Fort Bridger and around, over rugged gorges, down steep hills, and passages of very rough canons, making by that route, at least 15 days longer, and with all its perils, certainly renders this worth the deprivation.

"Quite a sandy & dusty trail; the first few miles level, latter part rolling, and perfectly arid. White clay formation. Dusty sage bush scattered over the country. And hosts of dead oxen.

"About Sun-Set a mule … next to rear failed, he had been sick, and we left him to the tender mercies of the wolves … Another mule fell, in harness, and finding that plunging the blade of a penknife into his shoulder created no sensation, we left him also, as a tribute to the lean lank wolves.

"Aug 5. — At 1 a.m., having driven 17 miles without water, halted to rest … Gave each mule 1 quart of water. Some of us eat a hasty bite of bread, but many were too fatigued to do that, and were all soon down under and about the wagons, rolled up in their blankets, in the deep dust — *dust to dust* — and soon sound asleep.

"About 4 a.m. we were again en route, on our thirsty and dusty route."

Along the route of the Sublette Cutoff on the way to rejoining the main path of the Oregon Trail.

"YOU HAVE NO IDEA OF THE CONFUSION AND UNCERTAINTY IN THE MINDS OF THE EMIGRANTS AS TO WHICH WAS THE BEST ROUTE TO TAKE …. ALL SORTS OF REPORTS WERE CIRCULATED. SOME SAID YOU HAD TO BUY THE LAND IN CALIFORNIA WHILE IN OREGON IT WAS FREE …. SOME ADVISED US TO TAKE THE SHORT CUT ACROSS THE 45-MILE DESERT, AVOIDING GOING TO FORT BRIDGER."

— *Lucy Ann Henderson Deady, 11 years old when she traveled the trail in 1846.*

THE MORMON TRAIL

Seeking a new home in the west, members of the Church of Jesus Christ of Latter-Day Saints sent out an advance party of 148 emigrants in spring 1847. This Pioneer Band left the Mormons' winter quarters near present-day Omaha and followed the north bank of the Platte River to Fort Laramie, where it proceeded along the Oregon Trail across the Rockies to Fort Bridger. From there, the party headed southwest and came on the basin of the Great Salt Lake. Leader Brigham Young pronounced it suitable both for productive land and isolation from other Americans. More than 1,500 Mormons made the trek that year, followed by 2,500 more in 1848, and their new home was secure.

BEAR RIVER VALLEY

> WE PASSED TODAY THE CELEBRATED BEER OR SODA SPRINGS. THERE IS OVER A HUNDRED OF THEM. THEY ARE ON THE BANK OF THE BEAR RIVER. THE WATER, WHEN YOU FIRST DIP IT UP, SPARKLES AND FOAMS THE SAME AS SODA. IT ALSO TASTES LIKE SODA WATER, ONLY A GREAT DEAL STRONGER."
>
> *– Joseph Hackney, 1849*

From Fort Bridger or the Sublette Cutoff, the emigrants on the Oregon Trail pushed on, heading north by northwest, over Oyster Ridge, across Muddy Creek, then Thomas Fork, and into the Bear River Valley. The wagons were moving into what today is southeastern Idaho.

What they saw ahead were huge hills, ones that a century and a half ago had to be attacked head on — straight up and straight down because wagon construction then didn't allow for much cornering ability. Get one side's wheels lower than the other and the whole top-heavy rig would fall over.

The worst hill of all was called simply Big Hill. Explorer John Charles Fremont, usually blase about topography, called Big Hill "a very steep, bad mountain."

Once down, though, the emigrants got a breather. The Bear River valley was an oasis, one full of sweet water, abundant grass and wood for cook fires.

Fremont saw this here in 1843:

"We descended into a beautiful bottom, formed by a lateral valley, which presented a picture of home beauty that went directly to our hearts.

"The edge of the wood, for several miles along the river, was dotted with the white covers of emigrant wagons ... where the smokes were rising lazily from the fires, around which the women were occupied in preparing the evening meal, and the children playing in the grass; and herds of cattle grazing about the bottom, had an air of quiet security, and civilized comfort, that made a rare sight for a

1,050 MILES

Facing page: *When they reached the Bear River, Oregon wagon trains passed the final Rocky Mountain portion of their voyage.*

Bear River Valley

traveller in such a remote wilderness."

It was on the Bear, in the late 1840s, that emigrants could replace their worn livestock at a place alternately known as Fort Smith, Big Timbers, Smith's Trading Post, all one and the same, all operated by William "Peg-Leg" Smith.

Smith was a Kentucky kid, a runaway to the mountains, becoming a trapper, mountain man, hard drinker, and husband of many Indian wives. Peg-Leg got his sobriquet in 1827 at age 26 when a Crow Indian shot him in the leg in northern Colorado. There was no hope for the limb, and it was amputated. Shortly thereafter, recovered, Smith carved himself a prosthesis and lived 39 more years.

For the emigrants who passed Smith's operation, the hard times were temporarily behind — desert east of the Green River; endless ridges north of Fort Bridger, jagged land along the east bank of the Bear.

And they needed a break. Ahead lay the Snake River, which would lead them across what today is southern Idaho.

By the 20th century a veritable garden because of irrigation, the Snake River Valley the emigrants experienced was a wild, living thing boiling through a rift cleaved through the hot, dry, and all but treeless land.

They would have another chance to be tourists, stopping by the Steamboat Springs, so called for its puffing. In the 1843 group, Overton Johnson said it tossed water into the air every 15 seconds.

Not far away was Soda Springs, where the water was imagined by trappers, too-long removed from civilization, to taste like beer. "We used this water in making our bread," recalled one of the 1845 emigrants.

But emigrants knew that unpleasant things were ahead, too: problems getting water up from stretches of the Snake gorge and voracious mosquitoes many would mention in their diaries.

And later, in the 1850s, the land along the Snake would present another problem — Indians who found wagon trains tempting targets.

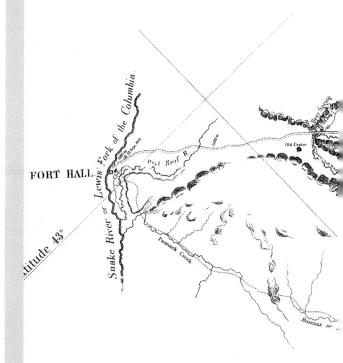

Fremont's route along the Bear River Valley and from it to Fort Hall and the Snake River.

Bear River Valley

"Great efforts were made to induce the emigrants to pursue the route to California. The most extravagant tales were related respecting the dangers that awaited a trip to Oregon."

— Joel Palmer, 1845

1,200 MILES

Fort Hall

Built in the early 1830s by an American who hoped to profit by selling goods to fur trappers, this trading trading post was sold in 1837 to the British Hudson's Bay Co. In the 1840s Fort Hall, like Laramie and Bridger before it and the Whitman mission to come, was an important supply point for emigrants to Oregon. It stood near where the trail met the Snake River, which the wagon trains would follow for many miles. The original structure was made of logs, and adobe brick was added after the British took over.

INDIANS

The Oregon Trail is "an astounding human achievement," acknowledges Joseph Marshall of Casper, Wyo., a historian, writer and Lakota Sioux. After all, tens of thousands people launched themselves across 2,000 miles.

"But there needs to be an understanding of what happened on the other side — the Indian side," Marshall says. "This was not an empty land. It was inhabited. It was used. It was home for a lot of people who were different than those people who came up the trail.

"To put it mildly, that migration raised havoc," he said. "But you rarely hear that when people talk about the trail."

The Oregon Trail was a visible manifestation of the ending of the nomadic way of life for the Plains and Rocky Mountain Indians. It brought sickness. It brought whiskey. It brought settlers who demanded that the military come along and protect them and "chastise the Indians" who "stood in the way of progress."

It eventually brought the railroads.

It brought killing, both of whites and Indians. And it brought about the slaughter of that staple of Indian life, the buffalo.

What happened to Indians in 1843 at Fort Hall would rarely, if ever, be mentioned by the chroniclers and historians of the trail.

For the first time, a large group of emigrants had taken over a wintering ground of Indian tribes, specifically the Shoshones, Bannocks and Paiutes. Actually, ever since they'd crossed "The Line" from Missouri, the overlanders had been on Indian land. They had camped on it, cut its firewood, shot game along the way.

But Fort Hall was different, said Clyde Hall, lawyer, tribal magistrate of the Fort Hall Indian Reservation, and of Shoshone-French ancestry.

"The Indians were away hunting," said

"I HAVE CONTEMPLATED THE NOBLE RACES OF THE RED MEN WHO ARE ... MELTING AWAY AT THE APPROACH OF CIVILIZATION; THEIR RIGHTS INVADED, THEIR MORALS CORRUPTED, THEIR LANDS WRESTED FROM THEM, THEIR CUSTOMS CHANGED, AND THEREFORE LOST TO THE WORLD."

— *George Catlin, painter of Indian tribes, 1832.*

Indians

Hall, who was interviewed in the 1990s. "When they came back in the fall, their grass was eaten, the game was scarce, the marks of the white man were all around."

The 800-odd members of the 1843 train, the first large one along the trail, probably didn't do much harm. But in the ensuing years Fort Hall became a focus for the emigrants as the trail became crowded with settlers headed for Oregon and later gold-seekers rushing to California. The damage became cumulative as thousands upon thousands passed through.

The region had been a virtual Eden where game abounded, huge trout swam in the crystal-clear waters, grass grew for Indians' ponies, and firewood was available.

Before too many years passed the land was stripped, the game vanished and the Indians saw nothing but the crowded fort and their own people becoming increasingly dependent on the white traders.

Occasionally emigrants left behind a lame cow or mule, maybe some thrown-away cookware. But they were gone, far down the trail by the time the Indians returned from their hunt.

"At first the Indians were puzzled," said Hall. "Where were all these people going in such a purposeful way? They were traveling to one point. The Indians, who traveled, but not like that, couldn't understand that."

With their wintering grounds befouled, Hall said, resentment grew among the Indians. Finally, in the 1860s they lashed out. Whites would call what happened massacres or depredations. Indians would call it self-defense.

In his book *The Plains Across*, John D. Unruh Jr. cites examples of blasting away at Indians who had done the emigrants no harm.

"One 1851 emigrant who was missing a horse, presumably due to Indian thievery, resolved to kill the next Indian he saw," Unruh writes. "He did — shooting from behind a rock an unsuspecting Indian who was busily spearing a salmon in the Snake River."

Loren Hastings, going through Pawnee country in 1847, wrote: "The best way, I think, to civilize or Christianize Indians is with powder & lead, & this the way we shall do hereafter."

The sentiment would be echoed again and again in later years as the emigrants and Indians crossed paths — often fatally for both.

"I LOVE THE LAND AND THE BUFFALO AND I WILL NOT PART WITH ANY ... I LOVE TO ROAM OVER THE WIDE PRAIRIE AND WHEN I DO, I FEEL FREE AND HAPPY, BUT WHEN WE SETTLE DOWN WE GROW PALE AND DIE."

— *Satanta, Kowa chief, October 1867.*

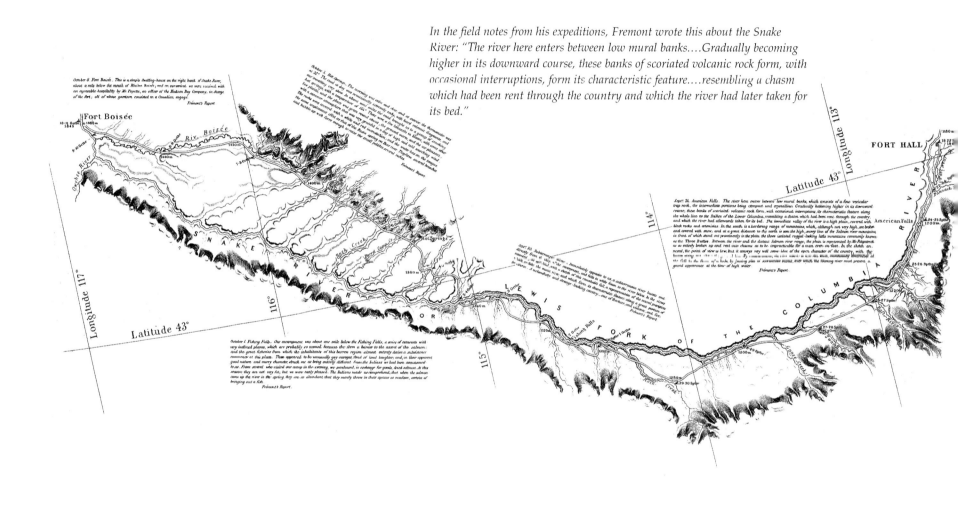

In the field notes from his expeditions, Fremont wrote this about the Snake River: "The river here enters between low mural banks....Gradually becoming higher in its downward course, these banks of scoriated volcanic rock form, with occasional interruptions, form its characteristic feature....resembling a chasm which had been rent through the country and which the river had later taken for its bed."

Snake River

> "Camped on Snake River. Plenty grass and willows. Very dusty roads. You in the States know nothing about dust. It will fly so that you can hardly see the horns of your tongue yoke. It often seems that the cattle must die for the want of breath, and then in our wagons such a spectacle, beds, cloths, victuals, and children, all completely covered."
>
> – Elizabeth Dixon Smith, 1847

The trail along the Snake River was a hard road for the Oregon emigrants, their path leading along a 300-mile stretch of sand, billowing dust, occasional mud and hungry mosquitoes.

What was maddening was that water — their one, absolute necessity — was just off the trail where the nearby Snake roared and tumbled down a deep, mostly inaccessible gorge.

Getting to that water was an ordeal. It was so close, yet so far.

Theodore Talbot, a member of the 1843 wagon train:

"To reach the water we have to follow a path nearly a mile long winding down the face of the cliff. Snake River, along here for miles, is walled in by high, perpendicular, basaltic bluffs. The river is … below the general level of the country, which consists of barren rock partly covered with sand and patches of absinthe. You may ride up to the brink of the

The Snake River

SNAKE RIVER

chasm through which the river flows without being aware of its existence."

Water wasn't the only problem, writes Lloyd W. Coffman, whose study of that 1843 wagon train indicated that the sagebrush covering the desert land was bigger and tougher than any seen so far.

Five wagons had to travel abreast to crush the sagebrush down for the following wagons. And every so often, those five had to be relieved with new teams, wagons and drivers. The going was that tough.

And when it rained, the trails became a quagmire. Some days were bitingly cold. Grass was scarce and food was running low. What helped were the Indians fishing for salmon in the river. For a price, they would part with some of their catch.

Explorer John Charles Fremont, following the 1843 emigrants, noted in his journal:

"Now we frequently saw Indians.... Very many of them were oddly and partially dressed in overcoat, skirt, waistcoat or pantaloons, or whatever article of clothing they had been able to procure in trade from the emigrants...."

With the dried fish traded from Indians, what water they could haul up from the Snake, and by putting one foot in front of the other, the emigrants kept going. They passed American Falls, went through what would become known as Massacre Rocks, crossed the Raft River where subsequent emigrants would leave the trail and head down another trace to California, and finally came to Shoshone Falls and Twin Falls.

The three waterfalls were landmarks for the overlanders. The roar of the Snake passing over them could be heard for miles.

"Much surprised to learn the next day that within 10 miles of this place there is a cascade which is not surpassed by the Niagara Falls...." wrote Osborne Cross on Aug. 15, 1849.

Preceding page: *Emigrants found the countryside of the Columbian Plateau, through the Bear River and the Snake River valleys, largely covered with sage.* Right: *Along the trail as it headed for Fort Hall.*

OFF TO CALIFORNIA

About 50 miles down the Snake River from Fort Hall, after the emigrants crossed the Raft River, travelers bound for California left the Oregon Trail and headed southwest for the Humboldt River. Until 1846, the number of emigrants continuing to Oregon Territory vastly exceeded those for California. Over the next three years, the numbers of each were roughly equal. But in 1848 word of the gold strike at Sutter's Mill changed everything. The next year, more than 25,000 people were estimated to have headed for California and only a few hundred to Oregon. Many goldseekers left the Oregon Trail before reaching Fort Hall and headed straight west to intercept the route from the Raft River. Over the next decade traffic to the Pacific Northwest would recover, but still pale compared with California travelers. In 1852, for example, 10,000 emigrants were estimated to have headed for Oregon but six times as many to California.

SNAKE RIVER

1,400 MILES

THREE-ISLAND CROSSING

Aiming to avoid a difficult route on the south side of the Snake River, most emigrants crossed to the north side at a spot with islands in mid-stream, left. In later years it was named Three-Island Crossing after a third island was formed. Some emigrants discounted reports that the crossing was hard, but others reported considerable struggle through a strong current.

Left: *Route of the trail after Three-Island Crossing.*

1,500 MILES

Fort Boise

The British Hudson's Bay Co. established this trading post where the Boise River meets the Snake River in 1834. Here, the trail crossed the Snake, far right on map. Like Fort Hall earlier on the trail, Ft. Boise was built of logs and later encased in adobe. Of it, Fremont noted in his report: "This is a simple dwelling-house on the right bank of the Snake River....On our arrival we were received with an agreeable hospitality."

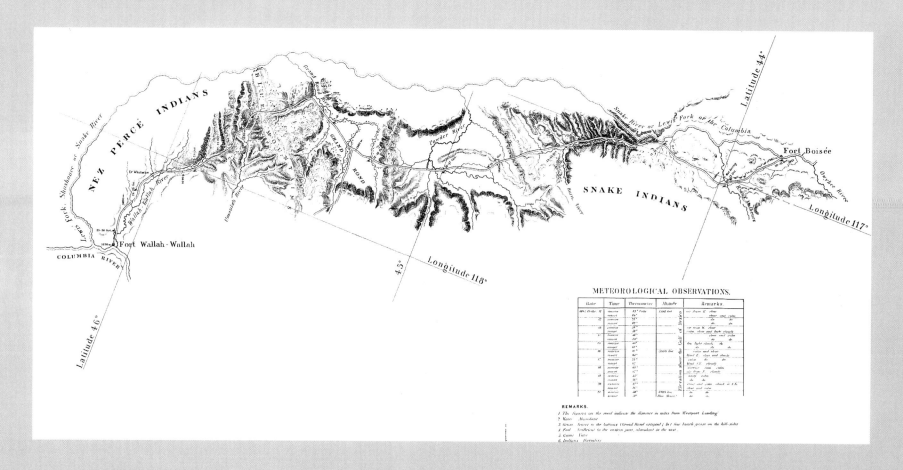

Blue Mountains

For Oregon Trail emigrants a century and a half ago, the journey that had begun with dreams and song at the Missouri River had turned — by the time they left the Snake River and passed through the valley of its tributary, the Burnt River, and faced the ominous Blue Mountains — into a matter of dogged endurance.

Beyond the Blue Mountains was either the rapids-strewn Columbia River or, starting in 1845, a fearsome trip through the fog and shadows of the Cascades.

By this point the emigrants were exhausted, their livestock thin and weakened, their supplies low and their dilapidated wagons barely resembling those that had rolled out of Missouri a scant four months before.

Like their wagons, the emigrants had changed.

Now their seemingly limitless patience was tested by the rugged ranges and valleys of Oregon.

Coming up the trail in 1852, John T. Kerns was not impressed by what he saw:

"Yo Ho. We are in Oregon. Me thinks this is not the place I started for and I will not be here long either, endured too many hardships and privations beside leaving a blank in my life."

Day after day of struggle, both in the Burnt River Valley and later the Blue Mountains, pushing, shoving, yelling at played-out oxen, fording and refording streams, hacking through woods, moving rocks so wagons could pass, losing cattle amid the thick pines. No wonder minds went blank.

1,600 MILES

> "SEPT. 24 — TRAILED 10 MILES OVER THE ROUGHEST COUNTRY I EVER SAW, BURNT RIVER BEING HEMMED IN BY HILLS ON BOTH SIDES. ENCAMPED IN THE BOTTOM.
> "SEPT. 25 — TRAILED 8 MILES. PASSED THE FORKS OF THE BURNT RIVER. THE ROADS ROUGH AND THE COUNTRY ROUGHER STILL."
>
> — *James Nesmith, 1843.*

BLUE MOUNTAINS

COLUMBIA PLATEAU

Once the Oregon Trail met the Snake River, travelers were out of the Rocky Mountains and crossing a vast region called the Columbia Plateau, with a topography dominated by lava from ancient volcanoes. Over the centuries, erosion had created steep mountainsides and deep valleys. Rugged as they were, the Blue Mountains featured thick timber and heavy plant growth on forest floors; otherwise vegetation across the plateau was scanty — largely sagebrush. Forage for draft animals was hard to find and water was often accessible only in streams at the bottom of sheer-walled canyons.

The Burnt River Valley, said John Charles Fremont, resembled "a hole among the hills."

As for the trace, Fremont said: "I have never seen a wagon road equally bad in the same space, as this of yesterday and today. I noticed where one wagon had been overturned twice, in a very short distance; and it was surprising to see that those wagons which were in the rear, and could not have had much assistance, got through at all."

Fremont was following the 1843 wagon train, which by now was more than 1,600 miles from its starting point, Independence, Mo.

Overlanders with that train agreed with Fremont.

"Terrible," Peter Burnett said of the road.

"The roughest country I ever saw," James Nesmith recalled.

William Newby, whose spelling is about as rocky as the terrain, recalled:

"We crawsed the river or creek I shall cawl it as it is a smawl stream. Dubeld teamed & crawsed the hill. It was a bout 3 quarters of a mile up & about the same down. Then we continued up the creek crawsing it some 8 or 10 times. Then passing through the hills whir you mite loock any way & it looked impossible for waggeons to pass we past with out much difficulty."

And those weren't even the Blue Mountains, which loomed ahead for some time, visually and mentally. Some emigrants reported being able to see the range from near Fort Boise. The missionary party of 1836 had been looking ahead toward those mountains when they finally abandoned their wagon cart at the fort, which itself would be abandoned 20 years later. Narcissa Whitman wrote this to family back East:

"Perhaps you will wonder why we have left the wagon, having taken it so nearly through. Our animals are failing, and the route in crossing the Blue Mountains is said to be impassable for it."

In 1843 the wagons would prove her wrong, but it wasn't easy because the timber, as Newby said, was "so thick in meney places that you coldant see a man 10 steps."

From this hill, about 1600 miles along the Oregon Trail, emigrants could get a good early look at the Blue Mountains lying ahead. The wagons are part of a display at the National Historic Oregon Trail Interpretive Center, run by the U.S. Bureau of Land Management east of Baker City, Ore.

BLUE MOUNTAINS

Ninevah Ford: "These hills were terrible. We camped many times in sight of our former night's camp. We found it very laborious and very hard cutting that Tamarisk timber with our dull axes we had not ground since we left Missouri."

So this part of Oregon was developing a reputation as a hard road. Yet this region offered two breaks from the back-wrenching work — the Baker Valley and the Grande Ronde (great round or basin) River valley.

Both had good grass and water. And, for a few hours, flat land to rest on. For some reason, neither valley would be populated for another 20 years.

The Grande Ronde valley was so wonderful that it made John T. Kerns eat his words as he descended a memorably steep hill into the mountain-rimmed basin: "This is the best and most beautiful place we have seen on the whole road, or in fact our lives, and is said to be a fair specimen of ... Oregon. If so, our expectations will be more than filled."

So why didn't they stop here?

"Traveling through this same part of the country many times since, I have often wondered why we passed by such rich soil and attractiveness and took up land in Western Oregon in no sense its equal in productiveness or health," remarked an 1852 overlander, Henry Gilfry, more than 50 years later. "The only reason I can assign is, we had started to go as far west as possible, and to the far west we are going."

Baker Valley was so treeless that it had a well-known landmark among the trappers, Indians and missionaries who had passed this way.

Lloyd W. Coffman, in *Blazing a Wagon Trail to Oregon*, wrote:

"The Lone Pine! It had stood for untold decades as a solitary landmark for travelers through the surrounding plain. Just the year before, an emigrant diarist named Medorem Crawford had written, 'The Tree is a large Pine stand(ing) in the middle of an immense plain intirely alone. It presented a truly singular appearance and I believe is respected by every traviler through this almost Treeless country.' "

Not all.

Coming into the valley days after the '43 caravan, Fremont looked in vain for *l'arbre seul*, "a beacon on the road for many years past."

"On arriving at the river," he wrote, "we found a fine tall pine stretched on the ground, which has been felled by some inconsiderate emigrant ax."

Burnett's diary agrees that one of his party had cut it down for firewood. Which was a futile exercise, noted Burnett, because "it was too green to burn."

The Whitmans

The name Whitman became almost synonymous with the Oregon Trail, especially in those early years when the track through the wilderness seemed all danger and travail.

For thousands of emigrants, Marcus Whitman, physician and minister, and Narcissa Whitman, missionary wife and teacher, shone like a beacon.

The two were overlanders themselves, messengers of Calvinist spirituality, keepers of a mission south of present-day Walla Walla, Wash., and finally on Nov. 29, 1847, victims of murder at the hands of the Cayuse Indians they were attempting to convert.

The killings catapulted the couple to martyrdom. The glory would transcend even the life of the trail, in books, paintings, even signs noting the Whitmans' first passage over the road to Oregon in 1836.

There was Narcissa, a heroine to women by the 1840s. One of the first two white women across the Rockies, she had charmed the raucous trappers at their Green River rendezvous. She also was a prolific writer, both of letters (many ending up in print) and magazines articles, and a role model for women considering the long trek west.

Not only had Narcissa gone up the trail, she had done it pregnant, jolting along in a springless wagon.

Yet the enthusiastic Narcissa would never be the same after 2-year-old Alice, conceived on the Oregon Trail, toddled down to the Walla Walla River and drowned in 1839. Narcissa began to take in other children, such as the seven Sager orphans, whose parents died on the trail, and the mixed-blood daughters of

"SOME FEEL ALMOST TO BLAME US FOR TELLING THEM ABOUT ETERNAL REALITIES. ONE SAID IT WAS GOOD WHEN THEY KNEW NOTHING BUT TO HUNT, EAT, DRINK AND SLEEP; NOW IT WAS BAD."

– *Narcissa Whitman, writing about the Cayuse.*

1,700 MILES

The Whitmans

the trail, and the mixed-blood daughters of mountain men Joe Meek and Jim Bridger.

And there was Marcus, who had set out to convert native Americans to Christianity but ultimately saw his future in provisioning the expanding waves of emigrants.

"Marcus enthusiastically supported the new course of events," wrote Julie Roy Jeffery in *Converting the West*, a definitive and critically acclaimed biography of Narcissa. "He wrote letters promoting emigration, and assisted weary and hungry families as they reached the mission. He had ambitious dreams for the future and saw few limits on Oregon's prospects."

"Marcus himself completed a new 'shorter & better' wagon route from the Umatilla to The Dalles," she wrote. Both Whitmans rode out to greet emigrant parties with food, and occasionally Marcus guided them. When rumors surfaced that some disgruntled Walla Walla and Cayuse might attack a wagon train, Whitman warned Indians that shiploads of soldiers and guns would come to kill all the Indians. One night, Jeffery wrote, Marcus held a chief captive and "insulted him by threatening to have him 'shot like a dog.' "

As early as 1837, Narcissa described herself in letters as being "in the darkness of heathenism." The souls she had set out to save had become people who were "full of fleas," "gamblers, adulterers and polygamists," "vain and never gratified."

Finally Secretary David Greene of the American Board of Commissioners of Foreign Missions warned Whitman about becoming a "man of business."

The board actually ordered his mission closed, but Whitman impetuously returned east to talk them out of it in 1842, then made his way back to the Northwest with one of the wagon trains. It arrived at the Whitman spread in early October 1843.

Whitman had been with that caravan much of the way, doing "hard labor," according to Peter Burnett.

In Independence the previous May, Whitman had calmed the fears of the emigrants who saw emptiness and privation when they looked west. He exhorted them to push out, take the new land and wrest Oregon from the British. At the crossing of Platte River in what is now Nebraska, he was there.

At Fort Hall, when some urged the abandonment of the wagons and a switch to pack horses, Whitman was there, too, insisting that wagons could make the trip. The emigrants again listened.

At Three-Island Crossing on the Snake River, Whitman saved the life of emigrant John Stoughton, whose horse had stumbled into deep water. Grasping the floundering animal's bridle, Whitman pulled it and Stoughton to safety.

And although Whitman left the column of wagons in the Blue Mountains to attend to business at home, his Cayuse friend Stickus guided the emigrants safely into the Umatilla River Valley and on into the mission. In 1843,

The Whitmans

Whitman was the indispensable man.

The attributes of both Marcus and Narcissa would transcend the years. The less-than-admirable points would fade. The emigrants of 1843 got a taste of some of the latter.

Whitman was a hard trader, according to emigrant William Newby.

"We lay buy within 3 miles of Doct Whitmans," Newby wrote, "a mishionary establishment to git provision … & the emigrant was much disapointed, as the Dr. had got them to come much out of there way with promices of provisions cheep, & was surprised by high prices we had to pay for all we got.…"

Peter Burnett defended Whitman, however, saying his cost of production was double what emigrants paid back in Missouri, which explained the doubled prices.

By the mid-1840s, Jeffery wrote, both the Whitmans had given up on the Cayuse. Little wonder. In 11 years, they had not converted one to Christianity.

The Cayuse were hunters and horse breeders, and they didn't take to horticulture. As a result, the missionaries came to think of them as lazy. But seeds of contempt had spread both ways.

Oddly, what had started out as a thriving mission had failed. And what had started out as a hardscrabble farm had flourished into a garden, a natural way stop for emigrants, especially the sick and hungry from disintegrating caravans.

So trouble was brewing. Narcissa wrote of threats as early as 1841. By 1847, friendly Indians, including Stickus, were warning the Whitmans of danger.

The flash point, most historians have agreed, was a measles epidemic at the mission, affecting white people and Indians alike. Although one white child died, most had some resistance and recovered. But 200 Indians perished, even after Whitman had treated many of them. They had no immunity to the disease.

The Cayuse elders came to the conclusion that Whitman was somehow poisoning the Indians.

They met him in the kitchen. One Indian struck him in the head with a tomahawk, another shot him in the neck. Narcissa, shot in the chest, was harbored upstairs but was finished off when lured outside. Twelve others were killed, and the mission was burned. Three sick children died because no one was there to tend them.

The Indians immediately took to the hills where they were hunted for years. Finally, five men gave themselves up and were hanged in Oregon City.

And the emigrants? They kept coming up the road. But at the Umatilla, they headed west to The Dalles instead of north to the Whitmans' place.

That made sense. There was nothing there anymore.

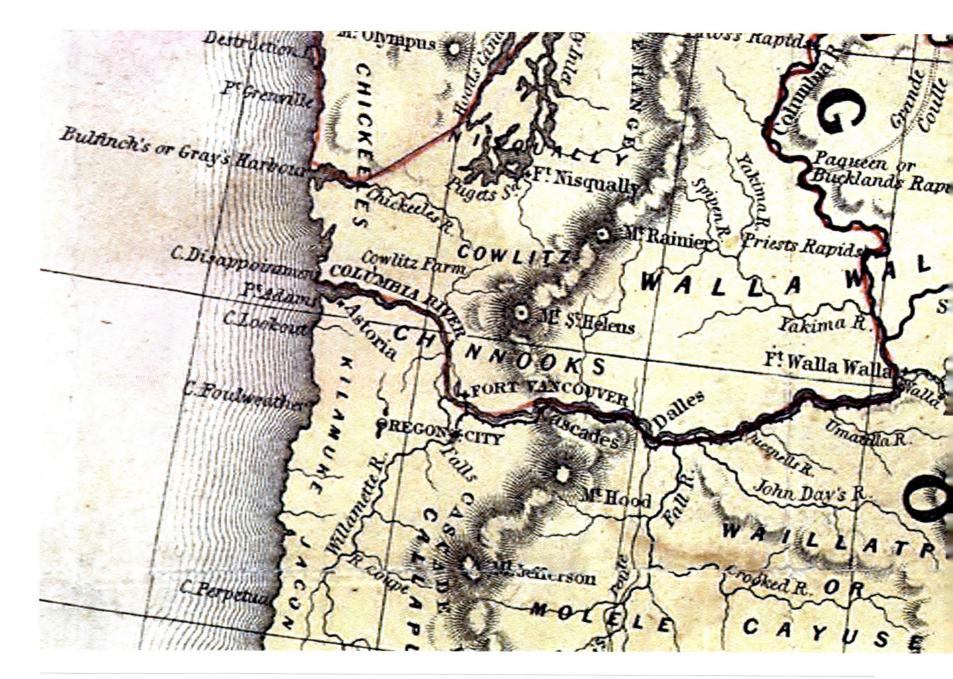

Augustus Mitchell's map shows the route from the Snake River to the Willamette Valley.

Columbia River

"Nov. 2 — We took off our wagon wheels, laid them on the raft, placed the wagon beds on them, and started. There are 3 families of us....The water runs 3 inches over our raft....

"Nov. 9 — Waves dashing over our raft....It is very cold. The icicles are hanging from our wagon beds to the water."

— *Elizabeth Dixon Smith on the Columbia River, 1847*

After five months on the trail, emigrants were exhausted. Many also were suffering from dysentery or fevers. So the idea of floating down a broad expanse of water was inviting. That's why many took to the Columbia River at The Dalles.

But the river, at first so placid-looking, became a thing where "the water foams and boils around ... like an enormous cauldron," wrote John Minto of the 1844 migration.

Aboard one of the boats built by his father and uncles, little Jesse Applegate, 7, would recall the horror of watching another vessel with family members aboard be swept into a set of rapids.

"Presently there was a wail of anguish, a shriek, and a scene of confusion in our boat that no language can describe. The boat we were watching disappeared and we saw the men and boys struggling in the water. Father and Uncle Jesse, seeing their children drowning, were about to leap from the boat to make a desperate attempt to swim to them, when mother and Aunt Cynthia, in voices that were distinctly heard above the roar of the waters, commanded: 'Men, don't quit the oars; if you do we will all be lost.' The men returned to the oars just in time to avoid, by great exertion, a rock."

Jesse's brother and cousin and another pioneer were lost.

At The Dalles, Methodists had opened a mission for the Indians. The French name means flagstones, logical enough to a traveler like Narcissa Whitman, the missionary wife from upriver: "Here our boat was stopped by

1,820 MILES

Facing page: *The Columbia River, more comfortably traveled in modern times than in the 1840s.*

COLUMBIA RIVER

two rocks of immense size and height, all the water in the river passing between them in a narrow channel and in great rapidity. Here we were obliged to land and make a portage of 2 and one-quarter miles, (Indians) carrying the boat also."

So at The Dalles the water-borne travelers had to stop temporarily to drag their jury-rigged vessels around the rocks. At that point overlanders could go no farther by land, at least until 1845, when a very rough road was blazed through the Cascades.

The obstacle was the Columbia River Gorge — a defile too steep, too rocky, too covered with moss, and too slick from seeping water and rain and snow to wrest an ox-pulled wagon across. With supreme effort, a man could make his way along the gorge, slipping and sliding. And cattle, with careful drovers, could manage the chasm.

But wagons? Impossible.

John Minto, descending by boat, went ashore in a storm and found a party of men and boys, trying to make the trip on foot with their cattle. The going had been so rough, Minto wrote, that "one of them had lost mental control of himself. He was not violent — just listless and helpless. The (others) had consumed their provisions and were separated from their cattle by a swollen stream and a dense snowstorm."

That's what the gorge was like. So the wagons that had brought the emigrants so far had to be disassembled at The Dalles and loaded on log rafts or boats for the final journey downriver to Fort Vancouver and then to the mouth of the Willamette River.

Little Jesse's uncle wrote later that subsequent migrations did not have it any easier at this point on their trip. Some of the emigrants in 1845 tried the north side of the Columbia and lost half their stock.

The older Jesse Applegate promoted an alternate route that left the trail hundreds of miles back at the Snake River and came down the Willamette River from the south. He had

More than a century and a half since emigrants began traveling the Oregon Trail, freight moves easily through the Columbia River valley.

98   2,000 MILES TO OREGON

Columbia River

little good to say about this river bottleneck in 1845, "the supply of boats being totally inadequate … and the stock of provisions failing at The Dalles, famine, and a malignant disease at the time raging amongst them.…"

Many families sat for days waiting for boats to become available. George Waggoner, who was 10 in 1852, recalled his father abandoning their wagon at the Umatilla and packing their bedding on their last ox, which they sold for $20 at The Dalles to buy food. To survive the two weeks there, his father found an old stove and cooked for the soldiers and civilians building a fort.

Nancy Hembree Bogart, who was 7 at the time, later recalled women in an 1843 party climbing aboard the flimsy boats and rafts that would carry them down the Columbia. They looked, she said, "as if they were facing death as never before."

"They took their places … looking stolid and indifferent, all their enthusiasm and finer feelings crushed out by the hardships already experienced."

Past The Dalles would be still more rapids and whirlpools and then one more portage around what was called the Cascades, a treacherous series of falls and rapids just east of Fort Vancouver.

"When we got to the cascades we had to unlode our botes and set up our wagons & and fill them and make a drive of 5 miles to the lower cascades. The botes were run over the falls and caught below by some Indians that were hired to look after them," explained Josiah Beal in 1847.

Assuming no capsizing and the cooperation of the strong winds on the river, the emigrant could move fairly quickly.

"With good connections at the six or seven portages, the float down to Fort Vancouver could be made in a day, but more often it took three days," says trail expert Gregory M. Franzwa in his *The Oregon Trail Revisited*.

In 1843, the emigrants finally reached Fort Vancouver, where they were greeted by Indians who brought gifts.

William Newby, a member of the always-hungry party, remembered long afterward: "Here they were gladdened by the sight of ripe, fresh apples which they had not seen since they left their far distant home."

It was just a little thing, apples. Yet for Newby and some of the others, that fruit would be remembered as long as they lived.

Of her new country Elizabeth Dixon Smith wrote this in 1847: "Nov. 20 — Rain all day. It is almost an impossibility to cook, and quite so to keep warm or dry." Fog shrouds the Cascade Mountains overlooking the Columbia River, right.

Barlow Road

The Oregon Trail, so near to its end, was almost more than the emigrants could bear, their diaries tell us. Especially those of the women.

"My husband is sick," Elizabeth Dixon Smith wrote in 1847. "It rains and snows. We start this morning round the falls with our wagons. We have five miles to go. I carry my babe and lead, or rather carry, another, through snow and mud and water almost to my knees. It is the worst road that a team could possibly travel.

"I went ahead with my children and I was afraid to look behind me for fear of seeing the wagons turn over into the mud and water with every thing in them. My children give out with cold and fatigue and could not travel and the boys had to unhitch the oxen and bring them and carry the children into camp.

"I was so cold and numb," continued the barefoot pioneer, who presumably still had to cook for her brood, "that I could not tell by feeling that I had any feet at all … I have not told half we suffered."

Not for nothing do the statues of the pioneer mother dot the cities along the western trails. They need one here on the old Barlow Road.

They and their families had overcome so much: the dust and heat across the "Great American Desert"; the passage through the Rocky Mountains; the continual search for the scant water and pasture for their livestock; the fording of countless rivers and streams; the worry about Indians and the bargaining with avaricious traders for precious provisions, and

1,820 MILES

Facing page: *The Barlow Road circled south around Mount Hood. This part of the trail was near Laurel Hill.*

> "MR. BARLOW IS ENTITLED TO MUCH CREDIT AND GRATITUDE … FOR THE PERSEVERANCE HE HAS MANIFESTED IN SURVEYING OUT AND MAKING THIS ROAD. ALTHOUGH WE ARE INFORMED THAT IT CAN AND OUGHT TO BE GREATLY IMPROVED."
>
> — *Oregon Spectator, Sept. 17, 1846*
>
> "THIS ROAD .. .WAS EXCEEDINGLY NARROW, FULL OF STUMPS AND OTHER OBSTRUCTIONS, WHICH MAKES IT MUCH THE WORST PORTION OF THE ROUTE FROM THE U.S. TO OREGON."
>
> — *Peter Burnett, March 1847*

Barlow Road

the illnesses, even death, of children and husbands.

Yet here, so tantalizingly near their goal, the very land, water and climate seemed to turn against them.

The final leg of the trip became a purgatory of fog and rushing waters; rain-shrouded, a seemingly impassable mountain barrier, and the coming snow across a dark, dank web of tangled woods and brush.

For the first years of migration, the problem at The Dalles, where the overland part of the trail ended, was threefold.

One was the almost palpable fear of the Columbia River with its rapids, falls and whirlpools, until then thought to be the only way to make the final leap westward to the Willamette Valley.

The second problem was time. Winter was approaching. Emigrants by the hundreds were at The Dalles, clamoring for transportation. But there were only so many boats.

The third was money. The emigrants had come almost 2,000 miles. The cash they had carried had been eaten up by bridge and ferry tolls, tributes to Indians and high prices for supplies at forts along the way.

And then, at The Dalles, what little money or goods they had left were being demanded by boatmen who wanted an arm and a leg as fare down river.

"On the verge of penury and treasuring what little capital they had remaining," writes historian Stephen D. Beckham, "few of the overland travelers were readily willing to pay for passage on that treacherous river."

That price, wrote Beckham, was dear: $50 for a wagon, and $10 a person. The tariff meant that the emigrant's cattle, herded west for months, would probably have to be sold. If they were flat broke, their wagon and some of their goods would go, too.

The question arose: Why had they come all this way, suffered such privations, and now would end up with nothing? Surely a road could be found.

Enter Samuel Kimbrough Barlow, 53, native Kentuckian and a man who typified the tough independence that marked the emigrants. Years later his daughter, Mary Barlow Wilkins, would quote her father as saying, "God never made a mountain that had no place to go over or around it."

The mountain, of course, was Mount Hood. With 13 wagons Barlow and Joel Palmer headed south and west from The Dalles, skirting the mountain's south shoulder. For two months they cut, burned and slashed their way over streams, up and down hills, through swamps and along razorbacked ridges. Winter came. They left their wagons in the wilderness and arrived in Oregon City in December.

The next spring Barlow was back for his wagons. He continued his road building and at the same time petitioned and received a charter from the provisional Oregon government for what would become legend: the Barlow Toll Road.

It cost $5 a wagon, 10 cents a head for cattle. They took barter, however — rifles or old quilts or anything else of value as payment, even IOUs from the truly flat broke. The toll angered other overland travelers, but it was a road, one that historian David Lavender said, "saved thousands of emigrants from the terrors of the Columbia."

It had terrors of its own, however. One traveler recalled:

BARLOW ROAD

"Some men's hearts died within them and some of our women sat down by the roadside and cried, saying they had abandoned all hope of ever reaching the promised land. I saw women with babies but a week old, toiling up the mountains in the burning sun, on foot, because our jaded teams were not able to haul them. We went down mountains so steep that we had to let our wagons down with rope."

Laurel Hill was one such hill. More than a century and a half later it seems unimaginable that anything — let alone a team, wagon and emigrant family — could have descended its several hundred yards of almost perpendicular rocks and brush. But they did.

Elizabeth Goltra wrote this in 1853:

"Sept. 24 — This is a rainy morning. The roads are very bad. Started early (and) got down Laurel Hill about dark. This is the roughest and steepest hill on the road. Got down by cutting & chaining a tree behind the wagon."

Another word about those women and those babies: Not only did many of the women on the trail bring along children, but most were pregnant on some part of the road and a great many went through childbirth before making Oregon.

Like the men, some broke under the strain of the trail. In her diary entry of Sept. 15, 1847, Elizabeth Dixon Smith told of a woman who refused to go any farther. Her husband kept the wagons moving, but sent back a son to check on her. Soon she ran up to the husband, exclaiming that she had dashed the son's brains out with a rock. The shocked husband ran back down the trail. Then he turned around and saw that his wife had set fire to the wagons.

He put the fire out, Smith continues, "then mustered spunk enough to give her a good flogging." The son, it turned out, was unharmed.

Smith is much admired by historian Merrill Mattes, who compiled a directory of emigrant diaries and wondered how she found time to keep such an excellent record while dragging eight children over the trail.

She recorded other women newly widowed by drownings or shootings (her own ill husband lived long enough to die in a leaky Portland shed) and noted that some of her

"TRAVELING THREE MILES OF 'BARLOW'S GATE' WHERE WE CAMPED....WE FIND NO ONE HERE TO TAKE TOLL AND THE POOR WORN OUT EMIGRANT IS NOT ONE BIT SORRY."

— *Enoch Conyers, Sept. 15, 1852*

BARLOW ROAD

party went to the Whitman Mission for help just in time to get killed by the Cayuse.

Meanwhile, the men who had probably made the decision to leave the Missouri or Illinois farm in the first place kept deciding to try new routes that got many killed.

One of the worst disasters of the trail occurred in 1845 after Stephen H.L. Meek persuaded 470 emigrants to branch off at Malheur ("unlucky") River into central Oregon, thus avoiding the rugged Burnt River Valley and Blue Mountains.

Meek, says trail historian Gregory Franzwa, apparently had never been up his proposed trail. Wagons went hub-deep in dust, emigrants sickened from mountain fever, cattle went lame or starved. Finally the survivors were rescued by the wily Moses "Black" Harris, a mountain man turned guide, who brought them to The Dalles.

"I will just say pen & tongue will both fall short when they go to tell the suffering the company went through," wrote Samuel Parker on Oct. 7 about "Meek's Terrible Trail." "There my wife and child died…."

Harris also would aid desperate travelers the next year on what was called the Applegate Trail, which attempted to enter the southern end of the Willamette Valley by traveling through far southern Oregon and northern California, then turning north. Although not the disaster the Meek Cutoff was, the Applegate route was a tough, dry route, where many cattle perished.

So most emigrants continued to use the Barlow Road, which became the main route of the Oregon Trail.

Vistas opened up as travelers on the Barlow Road neared Oregon City.

Trail's End

> "Passing through the timber that lies to the east of the city, we beheld Oregon (City) and the Falls of the Willamette at the same moment. We were ... filled with gratitude that we had reached the settlements of the white man, and with admiration at the appearance of the large sheet of water rolling over the Falls."
>
> – Joel Palmer, 1845

"The emigrants of 1843," the *Oregon Spectator* once wrote " ... though so near the end of their journey ... experienced far more losses, hardship and sufferings in descending from The Dalles to the Willamette, than in all the rest of the journey together.

"Almost in sight of the great object of their wishes, many were relieved from perishing by the benevolence of the Hudson's Bay Company...."

The company was personified by Dr. John McLoughlin, its factor and a friend to many of those earliest emigrants arriving sick, cold, tired and broke. He was the region's most famous resident.

John Boardman on Nov. 3, 1843, recorded the help of "Doct. McLoughlin, who charged nothing for the use of his boat sent up for us, nor for the provisions, but not satisfied with that sent us plenty of salmon and potatoes, furnished us house room, and wood free of charge, and was very anxious that all should get through safe."

McLoughlin's influence, which kept the local Indians from wiping out "the Bostons" (their term for the 1843 group), also went a long way in preventing war between the Americans and British over the area.

Actually, his British superiors were less than pleased by McLoughlin's generosity. Trail historian James Unruh Jr. writes of an 1845

2,000 MILES

Facing page: *Where upriver travel stopped: Falls of the Willamette at Oregon City, Ore.*

Settling In

"When he found a 640-acre claim on Mill Creek near Salem for which its ... owner would take $1,000, he bought it and moved mother at once into the double log cabin," wrote Mary Elizabeth Munkers Estes, who was 10 when she came overland in 1846.

"In addition to the cabin there was a log barn, ten acres of the 640 had been plowed and part of the place was fenced. My father had brought half a bushel of peach stones with him from Missouri. He planted these and soon had a fine orchard."

Not all were as well-off as Mary's family.

Here on the edge of the world, basic necessities were horribly expensive if they could even be found in those first years. Even cloth was impossible to find until someone brought sheep over the trail. Cotton could not be grown, so the women used the canvas from the wagon covers.

One of the Applegate women tried spinning a yarn from wolf hair. The younger Jesse Applegate would reflect later that "wolves could not be fleeced so long as they were alive and a man could not kill a sufficient number in a month to make a sweater."

Hezekiah Packingham wrote his brother that the country was "rapidly filling up with young men, of whom two-thirds are dissatisfied and many would return to the States if they were able, but the road back is long and tedious."

"Don't believe all that is said about Oregon, as many falsehoods are uttered."

investigative survey by British officers who contended that fewer than 30 American families would be in the area then if not for McLoughlin.

"Providing food to keep persons from starving was one thing," Unruh said, "but aiding citizens of a rival nation to found permanent settlements was another.

"Damned by the Americans who blamed the British for anything and everything, and damned by company officials for not more successfully resisting the American overland tide, McLoughlin could not win."

When the Barlow Road was finished, he resigned, moved out of Fort Vancouver and became a U.S. citizen, building a house in Oregon City. It's still there.

The emigrants, using the tools and seed wheat McLoughlin lent them, fanned out into the Willamette valley to take up their 640-acre claims. The seed produced a crop. In 1846 the provisional government declared a bushel of wheat legal tender, worth $1 a bushel. Three years later, when gold was discovered in California, Oregon wheat sold for $6 a bushel in

Trail's End

San Francisco.

The future of Oregon and the emigrants was assured.

For the emigrants spreading out across the valley, Oregon City was a way station. But with more overlanders piling in every year, it grew. For a time it was the state capital. It became the first incorporated town in this part of America, and the first to have a Masonic lodge, a library, a debating society, a newspaper and a temperance society.

Legend has it that Jesse Applegate, the St. Clair County, Mo., farmer, who came west with his cow column in 1843, replatted Oregon City a year after his arrival, using a rope instead of a chain. Naturally the rope stretched in Oregon's wet climate. No matter. Applegate marked off the lots that to this day are slightly bigger here, slightly smaller there.

Like Applegate, the majority of the emigrants who made it up the trial were from Missouri, according to historian John D. Unruh Jr. That finding was projected by Unruh from counts that show more than half the emigrants who died on the trail were Missourians and therefore more than half those who survived would have been too. Adding credence is that records of emigrants' passing through the toll gates on the Barlow road section of the trail show Missourians were the most common.

Oregon's 1850 census records showed 25 percent of residents said they'd been born in Missouri.

Within that 25 percent, 75 percent were dependents. What that meant, Unruh says, was that people born in other states ended up in Missouri, had children, then took off for Oregon — "a classic frontier pattern."

> "CAMP ON THE WILLAMETTE RIVER, THE HANDSOMEST VALLEY I EVER BEHELD. ALL CHARMED WITH THE PROSPECTS AND THINK THEY WILL BE WELL PAID FOR THEIR SUFFERINGS."
>
> – *Virgil Pringle, 1846*

James Clyman, a former mountain man and guide for early wagons, noted that even after they got to Oregon, many were still not ready to stop:

"Nearly all, like myself, (have) been a roving, discontented character before leaving their eastern homes. The long tiresome trip from the States has taught them what they are capable of performing and enduring.

"They talk of removing to the (Hawaiian) Islands, California, Chili , and other parts of South America with as much composure as you in Wisconsin talk of removing to Indiana or Michigan."

Historian David Lavender has a name for that desire to "remove" elsewhere, that itch to travel: "fiddle-footed." Lavender's term is rather odd, one afforded to people defined in their shining moment in American history.

The ocean stopped most of them. And they settled in to carve their mark on the land.

Next pages: *Near the waterfront where emigrants arrived a century and a half ago, fishing boats dot the Willamette River.*

Views on the Country

A strange land, without money or friends

Jan. 29, 1848 – "I sit up night after night with my poor sick husband …. He has not been moved off his bed for six weeks."

"Feb. 1 – It rained all day. This day my dear husband, my last remaining friend, died.

"Feb. 2 – Today we buried my earthly companion….. How comfortless is that of a widow's life, especially when left in a strange land without money or friends and the care of seven children."

— *Elizabeth Dixon Smith in Portland, Oregon country. Nearly a year and a half later, she would marry Joseph Cary Geer, whose spouse also had died upon reaching Oregon.*

Dried up and drowned

"My calculations are all defeated about Oregon. I found it a mean, dried up, and drowned country. ….. Corn, potatoes and garden vegetables cannot grow here without watering. The nights are too cold here in summer. The soil is not as good as in Illinois."

— *Hezekiah Packingham, March 1, 1847, in a letter to his brother.*

Times dull, money scarce

"We got here the 30th of August …. Times in Oregon are somewhat dull, money scarce. Land is all taken up that is worth taking …. There is a good many talking of leaving this country. I would not advise anyone to come here now."

— *Thomas J. Hayter, Sept. 23, 1854, in a letter to his parents in Missouri.*

Never going to leave

"Times at present are better than they have been for some time. I do not think, sister, I shall ever leave Oregon again as I enjoy better health here than any other place I ever have lived."

— *Thomas J. Hayter, April 21, 1856, in a letter to his sister in Missouri.*

Afterword

The influx of American settlers made it inevitable that the Willamette Valley and the region around it eventually would end up part of the United States. In 1846, Great Britain agreed to relinquish its claims south of the 49th parallel of latitude from the Rockies to the Pacific. In 1848, the U.S. portion became Oregon Territory.

Meanwhile, at the eastern end of the trail the Indian Territory of the 1840s was made Kansas and Nebraska territories in 1854. Five years later, Oregon won full statehood. Kansas entered the Union in 1861. In the decades after the Civil War, the remaining lands crossed by the Oregon Trail were admitted as states, first Nebraska in 1867, Washington in 1889, and Wyoming and Idaho in 1890.

Today, much of the remains of the actual Oregon Trail have been lost to agriculture or construction. Yet much of its path is followed by highways — a testimonial to the wisdom of the original route. Like the trail, Interstate 80 follows the easy grade of the Platte River for most of its way through Nebraska. In Wyoming, Interstate 25 parallels the North Platte for part of its journey. In Idaho and Oregon, Interstate 84 follows for many miles the trail's route along the Snake and Columbia rivers.

The last century has seen vast changes in technology. Americans on the move now travel in automobiles and airplanes; their possessions travel in trailers and vans. Ample food and safe, dry lodgings lie all along the way. Telephones and emails make communication instantaneous.

Circumstances have changed, too. Today roads west go through organized states, counties and cities, each with laws enforced by local agents, and lawyers to help people who are in trouble with the law or who have a grievance with other people.

What remains unchanged are human beings. As *2,000 Miles to Oregon* shows, trail travelers in the first half of the 19th century could be proud and happy, fearful and hateful, cooperative and divisive — just like human beings in the first years of the 21st century.

The differences between us and the emigrants, summed up in the overwhelming difficulties they faced on the way, make the story of the Oregon Trail compelling. The similarities between us make it spellbinding.

To Learn More

These books range from standard histories to detailed guides for finding the trail today.

■ *The Oregon Trail Revisited.* Gregory M. Franzwa first published this guidebook in 1972, updated it in the 1980s and thoroughly updated it in 1997. The 444-page volume carefully describes the routes the trail took from jumping-off points in the Kansas City area all the way to Oregon. It tells where ruts can still be seen, and supplies history and anecdotes through the six states along the route.

■ *Maps of the Oregon Trail.* Section by section, the 133 maps in this book trace the route of the trail in black over tan county maps. For anyone who wants to follow the trail, this is a helpful supplement to Franzwa's *Oregon Trail Revisited*.

■ *Historic Sites Along the Oregon Trail.* Aubrey L. Haines was contracted by the National Park Service in 1972 to study the trail and gather information on sites along it, and this book is drawn from that survey. In more than 400 pages it describes hundreds of sites, tells their distance from Independence and adds quotations from diarists and later students of the trail.

■ *The Great Platte River Road: The Covered Wagon Mainline Via Fort Kearny to Fort Laramie.* Merrill J. Mattes' topic is the wide, flat and much-traveled valley of the Platte River, used not only by emigrants to Oregon but also by California goldseekers, Mormons, freighters and the Pony Express. Nineteenth-century travelers used various routes to the Platte River and took various routes west upon leaving it, and Mattes discusses these, too. But the prime topic of this 624-page volume is the central portion of the route across the high plains.

■ *The Plains Across: The Overland Emigrants and the Trans-Mississippi West, 1840-1869.* John D. Unruh's fine research refutes trail myths and provides a deeper understanding of the West in general. The 592-page volume won seven book awards and was a finalist for the Pulitzer prize in history.

Photographs

All photographs by **Don Ipock** except as follows:

Monroe Dodd: x, 4, 4-5, 7, 11, 12, 14-15, 16, 19, 20, 21, 22, 23, 27 and 116.

Jean Donaldson Dodd: Pages v, viii, 14, 24 (top), 25 (bottom), 26 and 117.

Maps

- Library of Congress Geography and Map Division, Washington, D.C.

Other illustrations

- Kansas City Public Library, Special Collections Department: Page 3.

Acknowledgement

- Craig Crease of Shawnee, Kan., a premier trails sleuth in the Kansas City area, was kind enough to read this and offer valuable suggestions.

Reconstructed log cabin at Rock Creek Station State Historical Park, Jefferson County, Neb.

Pioneer Mother statue, Penn Valley Park, Kansas City, Mo.

No better place

"No single man should come to this country…. Nothing but men of families are wanted here to till the soil, to make this one of the greatest countries in the world. The good land in this country is more extensive than I expected."

— *Richard R. Howard, April 6, 1847, in a letter to a friend in Illinois.*